ENCYCLOPAEDIA OF EMINENT THINKERS

VOLUME-VI: AUROBINDO

Encyclopaedia of Eminent Thinkers Series

Vol. I. The Political Thought of **Mahatma Gandhi**
Vol. II. The Political Thought of **Nehru**
Vol. III. The Political Thought of **Rabindra Nath Tagore**
Vol. IV. The Political Thought of **Radhakrishnan**
Vol. V. The Political Thought of **Vinoba**
Vol. VI. The Political Thought of **Aurobindo**
Vol. VII. The Political Thought of **Jayaprakash Narayan**
Vol. VIII. The Political Thought of **Vivekananda**
Vol. IX. The Political Thought of **Ambedkar**
Vol. X. The Political Thought of **M.N. Roy**
Vol. XI. The Political Thought of **Dadabhai Naoroji**
Vol. XII. The Political Thought of **Veer Savarkar**
Vol. XIII. The Political Thought of **M.A. Jinnah**
Vol. XIV. The Political Thought of **Tej Bahadur Sapru**
Vol. XV. The Political Thought of **C. Rajagopalachari**
Vol. XVI. The Political Thought of **Subhas Chandra Bose**
Vol. XVII. The Political Thought of **Mohammad Iqbal**
Vol. XVIII. The Political Thought of **K.B. Hedgewar**
Vol. XIX. The Political Thought of **Bhagat Singh**
Vol. XX. The Political Thought of **M.S. Golwalkar**
Vol. XXI. The Political Thought of **Sir Syed Ahmed Khan**
Vol. XXII. The Political Thought of **Mahadev Govind Ranade**
Vol. XXIII. The Political Thought of **Pandit Deendayal Upadhyaya**
Vol. XXIV. The Political Thought of **Lokmanya Bal Gangadhar Tilak**
Vol. XXV. The Political Thought of **Annie Besant**
Vol. XXVI. The Political Thought of **C.R. Das**
Vol. XXVII. The Political Thought of **Gopal Krishna Gokhale**
Vol. XXVIII. The Political Thought of **Lala Lajpat Rai**
Vol. XXIX. The Political Thought of **Maulana Abul Kalam Azad**
Vol. XXX. The Political Thought of **Sir Pherozeshah Mehta**

About the Author

K.S. Bharathi did his Master's Degree in Gandhian Thought, Peace-Science, Economics, and political Science. He also did Postgraduate Diplomas in Politics, Public Administraion, Population Dynamics, Gandhian Thought, Tourism, and Telgu. He has contributed some articles in learned journals. He is the author of : *Foundation of Gandhian Thought Gandhi and Humanity, Socio Religious Thoughts of Mahatma Gandhi, The philosophy of Sarvodya, The Satyagraha of Mahatma Gandhi, Gandhi and Nehru, Foundatoins of Ambedkar Thought, The Social Philosophy of Mahatma Gandhi, Gandhian Approach to Rural Development, The Relevance of Gandhi, Gandhi and Vinoba, The Philosophical Foundations of Gandhian Thought, The Political Thought of Gandhi, The Economic Thought of Gandhi, The Social Thought of Gandhi* and *The Quintessence and Chronology of Gandhi*. At present, he is the Head of the Postgraduate Department of Gandhian Thought of Nagpur University. He is the Chairman of the Board of Studies of Gandhian Thought, member of the Academic Council, member of the Faculty of Social Science, member of the Board of Examination, and member of the Doctoral Research Committee of Nagpur University.

ENCYCLOPAEDIA OF EMINENT THINKERS

VOLUME-SIX

THE POLITICAL THOUGHT OF AUROBINDO

K.S. BHARATHI
Head, P.G. Department of Gandhian Thought,
Nagpur University, Nagpur

CONCEPT PUBLISHING COMPANY PVT. LTD.
NEW DELHI-110059

ISBN: 978-81-7022-707-6 (Vol. 6)
ISBN: 978-81-7022-684-0 (Series)

First Published 1998

Published and Printed by

Concept
Since 1974

Concept Publishing Company Pvt. Ltd.
A/15-16, Commercial Block, Mohan Garden,
New Delhi-110059 (India)
T: 91-11-41101460
E: publishing@conceptpub.com, *W*: www.conceptpub.com

DEDICATED TO MY FATHER

K.R. SWAMI

PREFACE

There are many valuable books on Aurobindo. There is hardly any book attempting a comprehensive exposition and evaluation of the political thought of Aurobindo. This work seeks to provide a comprehensive exposition of the Political Thought of Aurobindo in a lucid manner.

Aurobindo is physically no more with us, but still he is present amongst us not only as a consciousness which guides and illumines but also as a dynamic presence in action. He is not a political thinker in the ordinary and limited sense of the word since his political thought is an integral part of his overall vision of Reality. The political thought of Aurobindo is an amalgam of religion, metaphysics, psychology and prophecy and cannot be considered in isolation from its affiliation above four subjects.

This book is an attempt to reconstruct and critically evaluate the political thought of Aurobindo. His political writings are significant not only because he was a great leader but also because they are imbued with the spirit of exalted patriotic fervour. He has taught the gospel of one world and the inner oneness of man in his *Ideal of Human Unity* book. His *Human Cycle* enunciates a psychological and metaphysical approach to the study of the evolution of human civilisation and culture.

I would like to place on record my indebtedness to scholars and thinkers whose ideas enabled me to bring out this book. I gratefully acknowledge the scholars from whose works I have drawn citations viz. Dr. V.P. Varma, Dr. Haridas Chauduri, Dr. S.P. Ranchan, Dr. S.L. Mukherjee, Dr. Kishore and Shri Aurobindo.

So far as the writing of this book is concerned, whatever success I have achieved is due to the relentless efforts and encouragement of my friend, philosopher and guide, Dr. P.S.G. Kumar, Head, Department of Library and Information Science, Nagpur University. I sincerely express my gratitude to him.

I express my warm thanks to Shri P.N. Hardas of Gandhian Thought Department, Nagpur University for his help and cooperation provided to me in the completion of this work.

I am indebted to Ashok Kumar Mittal, Concept Publishing Company for publishing this book in such a short span of time. Finally I hold myself to blame for the errors and shortcomings if any. This work would have not been completed without the grace of Lord Venkateswara of Tirumala and Alamelu Thayar of Tiruchanur.

K.S. BHARATHI

CONTENTS

1

LIFE AND WORK OF AUROBINDO

Among the contemporary humanists of India Sri Aurobindo occupies a unique place of honour and reverence. He belongs to all nations and all sages, eternal or *sanatana* in character. Unlike Mahatma Gandhi and Tagore he could not influence vast masses. Even then those who care to go through his teachings are bound to note his burning optimism about the future of the human race. His realistic approach to the problems of life and his grand vision of human perfectability give a new hope to the bewildered mankind.

Aurobindo was one of the most creative and significant figures in the Indian *renaissance* movement. He was gifted with surprising powers of intellect and wisdom. In him, we find a synthesis of varied thoughts, and it is difficult to understand his thought-system unless we take an integrated view of human knowledge and human life. Romain Rolland regarded him as the highest synthesis of the *genius* of Europe and the genius of Asia. Tagore hailed him as the most pronounced exponent of the spiritual message of India to the world. Dr. Radhakrishnan considered him perhaps the most accomplished of modern Indian thinkers and in a statement to the press after Aurobindo's death declared him to be the greatest intellectual of our age.

Aurobindo is a poet of the cosmic drama, and a great master of style. He is a patriot and a lover of *humanity*. He is a *yogi*, a *risi*, an artist of illumined life. He is a prophet of supermanhood, and an architect of life divine on earth. He is regarded as an *avatar* who came to fulfil the divine purpose in the world by preparing the ground for fuller manifestation of the transforming power of the Divine in the sphere of evolution. He has given to humanity a new creative idea, and a dynamic world-force.

Aurobindo was born in Calcutta on August 15, 1872 in the Hooghly district of West Bengal. His grandfather was closely associated with the *Brahmo Samaj*. His father, Dr. Krishnadhan Ghose was regarded as one of the most successful civil surgeons of the day. He was one of the first few Indians to go to Britain for education. After his education he returned to India entirely anglicised in habits, ideas and ideals. He was a confirmed atheist and an opponent of every form of religious taboo and absurd customs. He was a great friend of the people, alertly responsive to the social and literary currents of his time, and an active bridge or link between the Europeans and the Indians. He wanted to give his children a thoroughly a European type of education. In 1879 he and his wife took Aurobindo and his elder brothers to England and entrusted them to an English family, the Drewetts, in Manchester.

Aurobindo was privately coached at home by Mr. and Mrs. Drewett. Mr. Drewett gave him a good grounding in English and Latin. Mrs. Drewett taught him history, geography, arithmetic. Aurobindo read scores of books on varying subjects and began writing verses for the Fox family magazine even at that early age. He grew up in entire ignorance of India, her people, her *religion* and her *culture*. He was deprived of the emotional warmth and bodily contact of his parents in his infancy and childhood. This resulted in unfavourable conditioning of his personalised emotions, behavioural pattern and archetypal images. He thus grew up in an emotional vacuum, which he filled up with objective, large, vast, linguistic, literary and historical interest.[1]

At the age of twelve, Aurobindo was sent to the St. Paul School, London. He proceeded to learn Greek. He was so quick in mastering the Greek language that the Headmaster of the School, Dr. F.W. Walker was taken by surprise. He was in this school for five years. He spent most of his time in the study of classics, besides general reading, especially English poetry, literature and fiction, French literature and the European history. He also devoted some time to learn Italian, German and Spanish. He achieved distinction in literature and history. He was awarded the Butterworth Second Prize in literature and the Bedford Prize in history.

In England, Aurobindo lived in great financial hardship on account of his father's failure to send remittances regularly. He said, "You will not understand me, unless I tell a circumstance of my life which is unhappily both painful for me to reveal, and for you to hear. I had no mother. She is insane. You may judge the horror of this, how I strove to snatch a fearful love, but only succeeded in hating and loathing, and at last becoming cold. Crying for bread I was given a stone. My father was kind but stern, and I never saw much of him. Thus from childhood I was subjected to fits of gloom and despondence which grew with my age".[2]

Aurobindo went to the King's College, Cambridge at the age of eighteen. He obtained a senior classical scholarship of the value of £ 80 per year. In King's College he obtained all the Prizes in one year for Greek and Latin verse, etc. His interest was not confined to classical studies; he made a deep study of the modern European history and literature. In 1890 he appeared for the Indian Civil Service Examination and passed it with credit, scoring record marks in Greek and Latin. At the end of the period of probation, however, he avoided appearing for the departmental Riding Examination. He felt no call for the I.C.S., and wished to escape from that bondage. He said, "It was partly father's fault that I failed in the riding test.... He did not send money and riding lessons at Cambridge at that time were rather costly".[3]

At the age of twenty, Aurobindo achieved rare academic distinctions. He passed the First Part of the Classical Tripos Examination in the first class. Besides Greek, Latin and English, he mastered French, and acquired sufficient familiarity with other continental languages like German and Italian. He was sensitive to beauty in man and nature. From childhood he had a strong hatred and disgust for all kinds of cruelty and oppression, and watched with abhorrence the thousand and one instances of man's cruelty to man. He attained considerable fame as a poet. He was also active to some extent in the political field. At Cambridge as a member of the Indian Majlis, of which laterly he became the secretary, he delivered many revolutionary speeches, stressing the need for India's attainment of political independence as an essential pre-requisite to the fulfilment of her destiny in the world. He was growing aware of the horrors of India's political subjection to a foreign rule.[4]

Inspite of a European upbringing and ignorance of the Indian languages and culture, Aurobindo could not remain uninfluenced by the attitudes of his parents. His mother was wholly Indian although unassertive. His father was every inch an Englishman but cherished noble ideals of patriotism and service of the poor. A true lover of his country Dr. Krishnadhan Ghose thought that the salvation of India would come about through the importation of the Western methods and ways of life. At times he protested strongly against the injustices of the British Government in India and conveyed his reactions to his sons in England. Thus it may be said that Aurobindo got the first lessons in patriotism from his father.

Aurobindo's fourteen years of stay in England was the formative period of his life both as a period of his intellectual growth and preparation for the life to come in India. It was in England that his desire to serve his motherland became explicit. His association with the Indian Majlis, a students association, and a secret group of revolutionary Indians known as the 'Lotus and Dagger' gave him ample opportunity to foster his patriotism. Some of his statements given in England against British imperialism could easily be characterised as *revolutionary*. This revolutionary fervour came out openly when he returned to India in 1893.

Aurobindo reached Appolo Bunder, Bombay in February,

1893. His father had died before his arrival in India. It is said that by some mistake wrong news about Aurobindo's death in some shipwreck was conveyed to him. It gave him such a shock that he could not survive. Aurobindo said, "Since I set foot on Indian soil on the Appolo Bunder in Bombay, I began to have spiritual experiences but these were not divorced from this world but had an inner and infinite bearing on it, such as a feeling of the Infinite pervading material space and the Immanent inhabiting material objects and bodies. At the same time, I found myself entering supraphysical world planes with influences and an effort from them upon the material plane".[5]

Aurobindo joined the Baroda State Service on February 8, 1893. He worked in the Survey Settlement Department, Stamp and Revenue Department and the Baroda State Secretariat. He drafted important letters of the Maharaja of Baroda and made digests of correspondence and documents. He even drafted agreements. He began to study vigorously. He mastered Bengali and Sanskrit so that he might go to the original sources of Indian philosophy. This was in a way the preparatory period of his politico-spiritual career. Though he was quite successful and had distinguished himself in the Baroda State Service, yet it was unsuited to his taste. His real interest lay in the pursuit of knowledge. Hence he became a lecturer's in French language at the Baroda College and was soon appointed as Professor of English. Later on he was appointed as the Vice-Principal of that college.

These were years of *self-culture*, of literary activity, and of preparation for Aurobindo's future work. He learned several Indian languages, especially Marathi and Gujarati, the two official languages of the Baroda State. He thus had the opportunity now of drinking deep at the fountain-source of Indian *culture*, and serving his country in various ways. A great part of the last years of his Baroda service was spent on leave in silent political activity, for he was barred from public action by his position at Baroda.

The seeds of patriotism were already sown in Aurobindo's mind while he was in Cambridge. After his return to India, he found that Indian National Congress needed reorganisation. He wanted to envigorate it for effective action. K.G. Deshpande who already knew him as high-spirited nationalist from his Cambridge days, requested him to contribute political articles to his *Indu Prakash*, a weekly, of which Deshpande was the editor. Aurobindo complied with his request and contributed a series of articles under the title, 'New Lamps for Old' from August 9, 1893 to February, 1894. These articles contained a severe criticism of the mendicant policy of Indian National Congress. Hence K.G. Deshpande became afraid lest he should be prosecuted for sedition. Consequently this series was discontinued. At Baroda in April 1901, he married Mrinalini, the daughter of Bhupal Chandra Bose of Jessore who had settled in Ranchi. He had happy relations with his wife, Mrinalini. But his busy political activities and other circumstances did not permit him to live with his wife for most of the time. However, his love and affection for his wife is evident from the long letters that he wrote to her. These letters contain a wealth of information regarding the inner development and politico-spiritual ambitions of Aurobindo.

Aurobindo wrote a booklet in 1903 entitled *No Compromise*, which was printed in secret. It created a stir in the political circles, in the right-thinking persons throughout the country. He advocated complete freedom for India in the Congress Session at Bombay in 1904. In 1904 he started the practice of *yoga* as he felt that it could be the only cure for his own deep-rooted sorrow and for the manifold ills of humanity. It was also the time when he felt that attachment to the world for the sake of personal comforts was one great obstacle in the way of attaining high ideals. In 1905, he wrote to his wife, "Our quest for happiness in this world reveals to us sorrow in the very midst of happiness. This holds good not merely in the case of attachment to our children but it is applicable to all our desires for worldly things".[6]

Aurobindo became conscious of his peculiar and extraordinary ambitions in life described as his three insanities. The first consisted of his faith that all things belonged to God and therefore man had no right to work for his own personal ends. The second consisted of the determination to see God face to face. For this personal perfection through *yoga* became essential. His third madness consisted of his love for the motherland. He thought that if he could not do anything for the elevation of his brethren in the country, he could do nothing for the rest of humanity.

The Partition of Bengal in 1905 was a blessing in disguise for Aurobindo to actively engage himself in the struggle for the Indian freedom. On April 14, 1906, he attended the Bengal Conference, which was declared illegal by the British Government. The procession of protest led by him was lathi-charged and many persons were injured. He was the first politician to stand openly for complete and absolute independence as the aim of political action in India. He contributed some of the opening articles to a weekly Bengali paper called *Jugantar* which preached open revolt, *guerilla warfare*. This temper of direct confrontation created a stir in the mind of the British people and they let loose repressive measures. The demand for *Purna Swaraj* could hardly find favour with the British rulers wedded to the traditions of autocracy.

Bipin Chandra Pal started a newspaper called *Bande Mataram* on August 6, 1906 and Aurobindo became its Editor. This paper contained a series of articles advocating the use of *swadeshi* goods, boycott of foreign goods, passive resistance, non-cooperation, national system of education, settlement of disputes in law by popular arbitration and other matters. Aurobindo attended the Congress session at Calcutta which demanded, for the first time in the history of the Congress, *swaraj*. In November, 1907, he led the Nationalist Party at the Midnapur session of the Bengal Provincial Conference and later its Hooghly session. He stressed for complete independence. He said, "A divine power is behind the movement. The Zeit-Geist, the time-spirit, is at work to bring about a mighty movement of which the world at the present juncture has need. That movement is the resurgence of

Asia and the resurgence of India is not only a necessary part of the larger movement but its central need. India is the key-stone of the arch, the chief inheritress of the common Asiatic destiny. . . . The idea of a free and united India has been born and arrived at full stature in the land of the *rishis*, and the spiritual force of a great civilisation of which the world has need, is gathering at its back".[7]

Aurobindo was arrested on May 3, 1908 in the famous Alipur conspiracy case. He remained in jail for one year. During this time he was drawn towards spiritual realisation. A decisive change came over him. The mystic experience in the Alipur jail made him to realise that he had been instrumental in giving a spin to the wheel of revolution. He decided to get away from active political life to immerse himself in *yogic* self-education and to prepare himself for the task of broadcasting the eternal message of India.

In the political field, Aurobindo tried to inspire his countrymen with new political ideas, and succeeded in bringing about a widespread political reawakening all over India by means of his powerful articles in various news-papers. He vehemently denounced the then Congress policy of prayer, petition and protest, and called for a dynamic leadership based upon *self-help* and *fearlessness*. He openly criticised the British commercial and industrial exploitation of India, and propagated the *swadeshi* idea of boycotting all British goods in favour of the products of indigenous Indian industries. He wanted to change the Congress from a centre of timid constitutional agitation into an effective instrument for revolutionary action, functioning self-confidently with its own resources and aiming at nothing but complete independence from foreign domination. He thundered forth the self-confidence of the younger generation, and the deepest aspiration of the soul of India—the aspiration for complete freedom.[8]

Aurobindo pointed to the disastrous effects of the British Imperialistic policy such as emasculation, stagnation or slow progress, poverty, economic dependence, absence of planned industrial development, etc. He further pointed out that even if an alien rule were benevolent and beneficent, that could not be a substitute for a free and healthy national life. He was not sufficiently long in the political field to carry through the ideas he formulated. But he had the satisfaction of witnessing a new spirit and a new awakening all over the country. In the Alipore jail he spent almost all his time in reading the *Gita* and the *Upanishads*, and in intensive meditation and the practice of *yoga*. He had the vivid realisation of the all-pervasive presence of the Supreme Spirit, permeating the whole of Nature and dwelling in the hearts of all individuals including even the most hardened criminals in the prison. His deeper yogic experiences more and more related him to the evolutionary drive of humanity as a whole or the fundamental drive of human civilisation, and finally to the divine will operative in cosmic evolution.

Through the competent handling of his case by the famous nationalist lawyer Mr. C.R. Das, Aurobindo was acquitted of the charge of sedition, and came out of the jail after one year's chequered experiences there. Defending Aurobindo, C.R. Das read from Aurobindo's statement, "The whole of my case before you is this. If it is suggested that I preached the ideal of freedom to my country which is against the law, I plead guilty to the charge. If it is an offence to preach the ideal of *freedom*, I admit having done it. I never have disputed it. I have adopted the principles of the political philosophy of the West and I have assimilated that to the immortal teachings of Vedantism. I felt I was called upon to preach to my country to make them realise that India had a mission to perform in the country of nations. If that is my fault you can chain me, imprison me, but you will never get out of me a denial of that charge".[9]

Aurobindo moved to Pondicherry and arrived there on April 4, 1910. He dropped all participation in public political activity. Several times he was invited to preside over the deliberations of the *Indian National Congress*, but he had to turn down such invitations in implicit obedience to his higher self-mission that had now been revealed to him. He visualised his own life mission as the task of dynamising the vast spiritual heritage of India and that of giving such a world-embracing and creative form to the spiritual way of living that a new order of human civilisation might grow out of a dynamic integration of the highest values of modern western culture and traditional oriented culture. His retirement to Pondicherry and cessation of all political activity did not mean withdrawal from life or the sphere of human evolution. Apparently isolated from the rest of the world, he maintained a close contact with the various movements of the world, acted from higher planes of consciousness, and cooperated with the creative forces of human history from a deeper perspective. He pointed out that the fate of India was indissolubly bound up with the interply of international forces, and that India must attain her *freedom* as a force for *democracy*, and not for *Nazism*.[10]

Aurobindo was able to realise his goal within a short span of four years by concentrating on *yoga*. He continued his practice with the same intensity until November 24, 1926. After realising his aim in 1914, he started a philosophical journal, *The Arya*. He published a series of articles on Essays on the *Gita*, The Life Divine, The Synthesis of Yoga, The Secret of the *Veda*, The Ideal of Human Unity, etc., in this journal. To quote Jawaharlal Nehru, "Aurobindo retired from politics after his departure to Pondicherry appears to be erroneous. He never left his interest in politics or political events. As a matter of fact, it is during this period (1910-1950) that his major works, which have a bearing on his political thought, came out. At the beginning of the Second World War, he actively favoured India siding with the Britishers against the *asuric*, Fascist forces. Again in 1942, he strongly opposed the '*Quit India Movement*' considering it inconsistent with the spirit of the times. It has, therefore, to be said that Sri Aurobindo had a solid connection with politics, and that this connection with politics was never severed even on his leaving for Pondicherry. In fact, it continued at a higher and deeper level so that he gives a political design to what the New World Order should be".[11]

In his own words Aurobindo said, "Let me tell you in confidence that I never, never was a philosopher although I have written philosophy which is another story altogether. I knew precious little about philosophy before I did the *yoga* and came to Pondicherry. . . . I was a poet and a politician, not a philosopher. How I managed to do it and why? First because Paul Richard proposed to me to cooperate in a philosophical review. . . and as my theory was that a *yogi* ought to be able to turn his hand to anything, I could not very well refuse; and then he had to go to the war and left me in the lurch with sixty-four pages a month of philosophy all to write by my lonely self. Secondly, because I had only to write down in the terms of the intellect all that I had observed and came to know in practising *yoga* daily and the philosophy was there automatically".[12]

Aurobindo described Pondicherry as his place of retreat, his cave of *tapasya*, not of the ascetic kind but of a brand of his own invention. The different phases of Aurobindo's life have been referred to by K.R. Srinivasa Iyengar in the following words: "The poet and humanist of the Baroda period gave place to the patriot and prophet and nationalist evangel of the Calcutta period, and he too gave place at the appointed time to the philosopher and *yogi* and pilgrim of *Eternity* of the Pondicherry period."[13]

Aurobindo handed over the entire administration of the *Ashram* to Mira Richard in whom he noticed a wonderful combination of rare spiritual insight and uncommon organising ability on November 24, 1926. She became the Mother of the Ashram, and he retired more into the background. Since that time he would appear in public and give *darsan* to disciples, admirers and spiritual seekers only on three or four special days throughout the year. Except on these days he would be completely inaccessible to the public. In the midst of absolute silence he was engaged with sustained concentration in bringing down into the flux of human evolution the creative light and transmutive power of the higher divine consciousness—the *Supermind.* He was also in close contact with the major cultural and ideological movements of the world, working upon them from higher planes of consciousness, in order to prepare the ground for an increasing transformation of the collective consciousness of mankind.

On December 11, 1948, the Andhra University awarded its Sir C.R. Reddy National Prize to Aurobindo as the sole sufficing genius of the age and as one of the saviours of *humanity* who belong to all ages and all nations. In the course of his message to the University on the occasion, Aurobindo briefly dealt with the significance of India's attainment of political independence, and also with the vast possibilities as well as the formidable dangers and difficulties that must be reckoned with. He sounded the note of warning that India should not yield to the temptation of becoming 'a nation like many others evolving an opulent industry and commerce, a powerful organisation of social and political life, an immense military strength, practising power politics with a high degree of success, guarding and extending zealously her gains and her interests, dominating even a large part of the world, but in this apparently magnificent progression forfeiting its *swadharma*, losing its soul. Then ancient Indian and her spirit might disappear altogether, and we would have only one more nation like the others. . . . at the very moment when in the rest of the world there is more and more a turning towards her for spiritual help and a saving light'. India should not, to be sure, neglect her material interests.

Aurobindo passed away on December 5, 1950. He left for the world a creative idea and a dynamic world force. The mother of Aurobindo Ashram announced that he had given assurance of his continued activity from higher planes of consciousness until human evolution blossomed forth into a new era of enduring *peace*, harmony and uninterrupted progress through a supramental change of man's collective consciousness. On April 24, 1951, the mother of the Ashram said, "Sri Aurobindo is present in our midst, and with all the power of his creative genius he presides over the formation of the University Centre which for years he considered as one of the best means for preparing the future humanity to receive the supramental light that will transform the elite of today into a new race manifesting upon earth the new light and force and life".[14] C.R. Das described him as the poet of patriotism, the prophet of nationalism and lover of humanity.

The political thought of Aurobindo can be studied from a large number of books written by him and the names of some of them are *The Human Cycle, The Ideal of Human Unity, The Ideal of Karmayogin, The Doctrine of Passive Resistance, Defence of Indian Culture, The Renaissance in India, Basis of Yoga, Riddles of the World, Synthesis of Yoga, The Life Divine*, etc.

The bedrock of the political philosophy of Aurobindo was his concept of spiritual nationalism and the divinity of the Motherland. He gave a radical philosophy to politics. He placed before the people the high ideal of *Poorna Swaraj* or complete independence. He made a great contribution to the theory of *boycott* and *passive resistance*. Another contribution of Aurobindo was lofty ideal of *human unity* and India's destined role in the international community. His ideal of human unity was one of his major contributions to modern Indian Political Theory. Dr. V.P. Varma said, "Aurobindo will be hailed not only as a mighty prophet of humanity, not only as one of the leaders of Indian renaissance and liberation, not only as a *Yogi*, poet, metaphysician and critic, but also a leader in idealistic political theory".[15]

REFERENCES

1. S.P. Ranchan and K.D. Gupta, 1988, *Sri Aurobindo as a Political Thinker*, Konark Publishers, Delhi, p. 2.
2. A.B. Purani, 1978, *The Life of Sri Aurobindo*, Sri Aurobindo

Ashram, Pondicherry, pp. 24-5.

3. *Ibid.*, p. 26.
4. Haridas Chaudhuri, 1951, *Sri Aurobindo: The Prophet of Life Divine*, Sri Aurobindo Ashram, Pondicherry, pp. 2-3.
5. Navajata, 1972, *Sri Aurobindo*, National Book Trust, New Delhi, p. 11.
6. R.R. Diwakar, 1967, *Mahayogi Sri Aurobindo*, p. 139.
7. Navajata, *Sri Aurobindo, op. cit.*, p. 26.
8. Haridas Chaudhuri, *Sri Aurobindo: The Prophet of Life Divine, op. cit.*, pp. 5-6.
9. Navajata, *Sri Aurobindo, op. cit.*, pp. 52-3.
10. Haridas Chaudhuri, *Sri Aurobindo: The Prophet of Life Divine, op. cit.*, pp. 9-10.
11. S.P. Ranchan and K.D. Gupta, *Sri Aurobindo as a Political Thinker, op. cit.*, p. 13.
12. Sri Aurobindo, 1953, *On Himself and on the Mother*, Sri Aurobindo Ashram, Pondicherry, p. 348.
13. K.C.S. Iyengar, *Sri Aurobindo's Life and Thought*, p. 126.
14. *Sri Aurobindo and his Ashram*, Sri Aurobindo Ashram, Pondicherry, 1951, p. 70.
15. V.P. Varma, 1960, *Political Philosophy of Sri Aurobindo*, Asia Publishing House, Bombay, p. 382.

2

AUROBINDO AND VIVEKANANDA

Aurobindo himself has described Vivekananda as a king among men and the leading exampler and the most powerful exponent of the philosophy of preservation by reconstruction, which is the essence of Sri Aurobindo's philosophy as well. He said, "The movement associated with the great names of Ramakrishna and Vivekananda has been a very wide synthesis of past religious motives and spiritual experience topped by a reaffirmation of the old asceticism and monasticism, but with new living strands in it".[1] Moreover, he publicly acknowledged that he was inspired by the vision of Vivekananda during his meditations in prison. Again, once at Baroda, when he was practising *Hatha-Yoga*, he perceived the presence of Vivekananda and felt as though he was keeping watch over him. He further acknowledged that these incidents and his teachings had profound influence on his life.

According to Aurobindo, Vivekananda is the architect of our national life; he is its chief leader. What was his ideal yesterday has become India's today. His *Vedanta* with its message of *abhih*, mission of man-making and theme of growth from within supplied the philosophical basis to the freedom movement in the post-1905 era. In 1915 he said, "Vivekananda was a soul of puissance if ever there was one, a very lion among men. . . . we perceive his influence still working gigantically, we know not well how, we know not well where, in something that is not yet formed, something leonine, grand, intuitive, upheaving, that has entered the soul of India and we say 'Behold, Vivekananda still lives in the soul of his Mother and in the souls of her children".[2]

It must not however be supposed that the philosophic outlook of Aurobindo was in no way dissimilar to Aurobindo. Dr. K.R. Srinivasa Iyengar said, "He (Aurobindo) had an immense admiration for Vivekananda and a much deeper feeling for Ramakrishna. But he did not altogether accept Vivekananda's philosophy or standpoint".[3] Although a *Neo-vedantin* par excellence, as he has been called by Romain Rolland, Aurobindo essentially differed from Vivekananda both as regards the conception of God and the view of *sannyasa*.

It is interesting to notice the affinity of reaction to political trends of these two personalities of renascent India. Immediately on his return from England in 1893, the year in which Vivekananda made his debut in the international arena, Aurobindo began attacking the Congress in a series of anonymous articles entitled 'New Lamps for Old'. He gave out in the third essay of the series that the Congress was not really national, because it represented not the mass of population, but a single and limited class. He said, "The Congress in Bengal is dying of consumption: annually its proportions sink into greater insignificance, its leaders. . . . have climbed to the rarefied atmosphere of the Legislative Council and lost all hold on the imagination of the young men. The desire for nobles and more inspiring patriotism is growing more intense".[4]

A few years later Vivekananda criticised in the same vein the class-character of the Congress which pretended to be national in its scope. He found the Congress organisation quite inadequate and alien to his scheme of 'national reawakening through the regeneration of the masses'.

Aurobindo found in Vivekananda a nobler and more inspiring patriotism which he was in search of. He further found in him the endorsement of his belief in the need for Purification by Blood and Fire, which can largely be equated with Vivekananda's renunciation and service. He said, "In Mr.

Hume's formation the proletariat remained, for any practical purpose, a piece off the board. Yet the proletariat is. . . . the real key to the situation. Torpod he is and immobile; he is nothing to an actual force, but he is a great potential force, and whoever succeeds in understanding and eliciting his strength becomes by the very strength the master of the future."[5] When he heard again and again Vivekananda's passionate plea for raising the masses, his belief, as mentioned above, crystallised into a conviction.

However, Aurobindo did not immediately chalk out a scheme for eliciting the proletariat's strength in the national movement, or, at least, could not put one into operation. This was perhaps owing to the fact that the tornado released by the partition of Bengal was not conducive to it, or it may be that Aurobindo thought some other methods more suitable for the beginning of the process of national salvation. He remained very much philosophical in his political outlook and came to furnish *nationalism* and kindred ideas with the much needed philosophical base, and in these Vivekananda's influence can be clearly traced.

Aurobindo preached with a true religious fervour that *nationalism* was a divine religion. He described it as a part of the struggle of the human spirit for emancipation. He said, "It is not in human nature to rest eternally contented with a state of subordination or serfdom. God made man in His own image, essentially and potentially free and pure; shall man keep him in eternal bondage and sin? *Freedom* is constitutional in man, and when this freedom is curtailed by social and civil laws and institutions, it is done not to kill but to perfect this very freedom itself. This is the only rational, justification of those necessary limitations that society imposes upon human freedom everywhere and where this justification is absent, human nature revolts against these limitations. . . . The desire for autonomy is constitutional in man and not a mere functional disturbance such as the tyrant or the aggressor has always proclaimed it to be".[6]

Freedom of the spirit implies not only inner freedom but

outer forms of liberty as well. In a word, it signifies full freedom that makes for the whole man. He said, "Three words have the power of remoulding nations and governments, *liberty, equality* and *fraternity*. These words, cast forth into being from the great stir and movement of the eighteenth century, continue to act on man because they point to the ultimate goal towards which human evolution ever moves. This liberty to which we progress is liberation out of a stage of bondage. We move from a stage of bondage to an original liberty. . . . This is what our philosophy suggests as the goal towards which we move, *mukti* or *moksha*. We are bound in the beginning by a lapse from pre-existent freedom, we strive to shake off the bonds, we move forward and forward until we have achieved the ultimate emancipation, that utter freedom of the soul, of the body or the whole man, that utter freedom from all bondage towards which humanity is always aspiring. We in India have found a mighty freedom within ourselves, our brother-men in Europe have worked towards freedom without. We have been moving on parallel lines towards the same end".[7]

The concept of full freedom, since it is spiritual in character, has its direction towards unity, seeking to establish its domain over the entire humanity. Dr. Iyengar said, "From the very first, the idea of personal salvation or of individual felicity did not seem to Aurobindo anything like a supreme aim, worth being pursued for its own sake; a solitary salvation leaving the world to its fate was almost distasteful to him".[8] He thus came to view *swaraj*, the ostensible object of his Nationalism, as the fulfilment of God's will. As late as in 1921, long after he had retired from politics, Aurobindo said, "The *yoga* we practise is not for ourselves alone, but for humanity. Its object is not personal *mukti*. . . . but the liberation of the human race".[9]

Aurobindo holds that liberty is in peril because of the absence of the sense of unity between individual and individual, between community and community, which pushes them to assert themselves at the expense of each other. He said, "If a real, a spiritual and psychological unit were effectuated, liberty would have no perils. .... for free individuals enamoured of unity would be compelled by themselves, by their own need, to accommodate perfectly their own growth with the growth of other fellows and would not feel themselves complete except in the free growth of others".[10] This proclamation of Aurobindo cannot but remind one of the cardinal social messages of Vivekananda's *Neo-Vedanta*.

So far as India was concerned Aurobindo perceived the basis of the unity to be spiritual in character. In other words, it is because of their innate tendency to conquer the inner nature that the Indian people have come to realise a oneness or a unity among themselves. It is again, as in the case of Vivekananda and Tagore, essentially a unity in diversity, which does not deaden the individual at all but makes his true freedom possible. He said, "The whole basis of the Indian mind is its spiritual and inward turn, its propensity to seek the things of the spirit and the inner being first and foremost and to look at all else as secondary, dependent, to be handled and determined in the light of the higher knowledge and as an expression, a preliminary or at least a pendent to the deeper spiritual aim—a tendency therefore to create whatever it had to create first on the inner plane and afterwards in its other aspects. This mentality and this consequent tendency to create from within outwards being given, it was inevitable that the unity India first created for herself should be the spiritual and cultural oneness. . . . It is due to this original peculiarity, to this indelible spiritual stamp, to this underlying oneness amidst all diversities that if India is not yet a single organised political nation, she still survives and is still India".[11]

In the revival of true *freedom* and spiritual unity the soul of India is to be rediscovered, and this Aurobindo thinks to be the key to India's emancipation and her social and political growth. Hence growth must be from within. He, therefore, passionately pleads for regional autonomy to permit the free play of individual and group *Dharmas*. Naturally he decries the base imitation of the West although his conception of the material and scientific conquests of Europe is complete. He said, "The lifeless attempt of the last generation to imitate and reproduce with a servile fidelity the ideals and forms of the West has been no true indication of the political mind and genius of the Indian people".[12] Elsewhere he remarked, "The nineteenth century in India was imitative, self-forgetful, artificial. It aimed at a successful reproduction of Europe in India, forgetting the deep saying of the *Gita*—Better the law of one's own being though it may be badly done than an alien *dharma* well followed; death in one's *dharma* is better, it is a dangerous thing to follow the law of another's nature. For death in one's *dharma* brings new birth, success in an alien path means only successful suicide".[13]

Aurobindo is not pessimistic. Amid all the mist of confusion he sees the possibility of a new twilight, not of an evening but a morning *yuga-sandhya*, when India would demonstrate that India of the ages is not dead nor has she spoken the last creative word; she lives and still has something to do for herself and the human peoples. Yet, he is clear that our *svadharma*—the law of our own being—must be reconciled with *yugadharma*—the mutation of the ages.

According to Aurobindo, fulfilment of India's nationalism clearly lies in her serving the entire humanity. His nation, therefore, as Romain Rolland puts it, 'was to be the servant of humanity'. It is *nationalism*, but nationalism of a different variety. It is a nationalism for extending life, not for diminishing it in any way. The essence of spirit is growth and, hence, when liberated, it knows no limitation. Liberated spirit works for the realisation of the unity of mankind on the basis of spirituality, not on the basis of politics or economics. This is another name of waking up the *atman*—the real self of man viewed both as an individual and as a member of a social group. Aurobindo said, "An awakening of the real Self of a nation is the condition of national greatness. The supreme Indian idea is the Unity of man in God, and the realisation of this idea, outwardly and inwardly, in social relation and in structure of society, are destined to govern all progress of the human kind. India, if she wishes, would lead the world".[14]

Aurobindo believed that India possesses in its past, a little rusty and out of use, the key to the progress of humanity and he hoped that it would be possible to polish up the key and put it to use again. It is by re-living the ancient wisdom of our scriptures that India would be able to fulfil her mission in the world. The past however was to be remade in the mould of the present. Preservation by reconstruction should be the keynote of the attempt. He said, "The traditions of the past are very great in their place—in the past. But that is no reason why we should go on repeating the past. In the evolution of spiritual consciousness upon earth, a great past ought to be followed by a greater future".[15]

The spiritualisation of politics, the interpretation of the soul of India, the call to wake it up through 'preservation by reconstruction', the belief in India's mission and the faith in its realisation—are in the nature of assertions by Vivekananda risen from the pyre, for one finds in these as in Vivekananda 'the same conception of the identity of India's national ideal and her spiritual mission, and the same *universal love*', and also the same forward-looking attitude. There is again, the reiteration of Vivekananda's assertion that our past was no doubt glorious but the future must be still more glorious.

Aurobindo practically names the same price for waking up *atman* in the nation and thereby realising its mission. He speaks of *self-sacrifice* and *service* which can be largely equated with Vivekananda's renunciation and service. He said, "The pride in the past, the pain of our present, the passion for the future are its trunk and branches. Self-sacrifice and self-forgetfulness, great service, high endurance for the country, are its fruits. And the sap that keeps it alive is the realisation of the motherhood of God in the country, the vision of the Mother, the perpetual contemplation, adoration and service of the Mother".[16] Chittaranjan Das described Aurobindo as the poet of patriotism, the prophet of nationalism and the lover of humanity. Aurobindo did not end in Vivekananda. He carried *Neo-Vedanta* towards a process of philosophic integration and came to his concept of a Divine Life realisable here on earth upon this bank and shoal of time.

REFERENCES

1. Sri Aurobindo, *The Renaissance in India*, Sri Aurobindo Ashram, Pondicherry, 1951, p. 46.
2. Sri Aurobindo, *Bankim-Tilak-Dayananda*, Sri Aurobindo Ashram, Pondicherry, 1955, pp. 41-2.
3. Sri Aurobindo, *Sri Aurobindo on Himself and on Mother*, *op. cit.*, pp. 41-2.
4. *Sri Aurobindo, Bankim Chandra Chatterji*, Sri Aurobindo Ashram, Pondicherry, 1964, p. 38.
5. *New Lamps for Old.* 6-3-1894.
6. R.C. Majumdar, *Freedom Movement*, Vol. I, *op. cit.*, pp. 423-24.
7. *Speeches of Sri Aurobindo*, pp. 93-94.
8. Ante, *op. cit.*, p. 119.
9. Sri Aurobindo, *The Yoga and its Objects*, Arya Publishing House, Calcutta, 1931, p. 5.
10. Sri Aurobindo, The Ideal of Human Unity, *op. cit.*, p. 166.
11. Sri Aurobindo, *The Spirit and Form of Indian Polity*, Arya Publishing House, Calcutta, 1947, pp. 68-70.
12. *Ibid.*, p. 91.
13. Sri Aurobindo, *The Ideal of Karmayogin*, Sri Aurobindo Ashram, Pondicherry, 1966, p. 22.
14. Romain Rolland, *Prophets of the New India*, *op. cit.*, pp. 502-03.
15. Iyengar, *op. cit.*, pp. 50-51.
16. *Sri Aurobindo, Speeches*, p. 82.

3

AUROBINDO ON INDIVIDUAL, STATE, DEMOCRACY AND FREEDOM

The individual is not a mere physical conglomeration and complex of material inconsistent force but is a spiritual soul, a being and self-expression of the universal and transcendent spiritual reality. The individual is a divine soul and the attainment of *spiritual freedom* and immortality is his aim. His destiny is the realisation of the essential unity of the *Brahma* and the spiritualisation of the terrestrial life, and not a sensationalistic and hedonistic immersion in the depths of material self-seeking and vital satisfactions. Aurubindo is opposed both to the materialistic and the sociological explanations of the individual self. He said, "No doubt what comes out in the individual and afterwards moves the mass must have been there already in the Universal Mind and the individual is only an instrument for its manifestation, discovery, development, but he is an indispensable instrument and an instrument not merely of subconscient Nature, not merely of an instinctive urge that moves the mass, but more directly of the spirit of whom that Nature is itself the instrument and the matrix of his creations".[1]

Aurobindo does not stand for the submergence of the *individual* in the larger social aggregations. The individual is a necessary instrument of the superphenomenal might and consciousness force of God. He said, "God having made man in His own image, with the ego as a centre of working, with the race, the collective *Narayana*, the *Vishwamanava* as the mould and circumscription, seeks to express in them some image of the unity, *omniscence, omnipotence*, which are the self-conception of the Divine".[2]

According to Aurobindo, the family, the clan and the tribe are based on vital foundations. The *family* is a larger vital ego and organism that invests the individual with some affectual and social responsibilities by making him a member of a competitive and cooperative life-unit. The origin of the clan and the tribe has its roots in the vital need of human nature for an associational corporate life, and the ready basis is given to it by the inevitable physical growth of the family into clan or tribe. His views about the growth of the tribe out of the patriarchal family is in line with the general conception prevalent among historians. He accepts the historicity of primitive commune. He said, "A cooperative form of human society existed formerly in the shape of the commune; but the restoration of the commune as a unit would imply practically the return to the old city state.[3]

According to Aurobindo, the society has a vital foundation. Like the family, the *society* also is a competitive and cooperative ego, only on a vaster scale. The families and the society provide for the collective satisfaction of vital needs, claims, interests and well-being. His view about the vital foundation of the society has also some Western parallels. He said, "Even the physical being of the society is a subjective power, not a mere objective existence. Much more is it in its inner self a great corporate soul with all the possibilities and dangers of the soul-life"[4]. He uses the organic analogy in his conceptual analysis of the society. He said, "The nation or society, like the individual, has a body, an organic life, a moral and aesthetic temperament, a developing mind and soul behind all these signs and powers for the sake of which they exist".[5]

Aurobindo draws a distinction between the natural or organic and the mechanised or rational society. The organic society arranges the mode of its cooperative behaviour and social interactions with reference to the general sense and instinct or intuition of the group life. The conception of society as an organism is also found in Tagore and Pal. The second type of society or the *society* in its mechanical and more rational form begins when political institutions are perfected more and more. Democracy and socialism indicate the stages at which the self-conscious evolution of society aims to attain quite a logical development. Self-consciousness can find its fullness of being and realisation not in the political society as T.H. Green thinks but in a cosmic consciousness.

According to Aurobindo, the individual is a soul incarnated for a divine fulfilment upon earth. The collectivity also is a soul-form of the Infinite, a collective soul myriadly embodied upon earth for a divine fulfilment. The society or the nation or other cooperative organic collectivities are sub-souls necessary for the complex manifestation of the divine. Each society develops a sub-soul or group-soul, character, type of mind and evolves its own governing and ordering ideas and tendencies that shape its life and institutions. The fundamental aim of society which is a group-soul or sub-soul is to make possible the progressive spiritual evolution of man. *Society* is a stage in the progress towards universality. To him, the divine perfection of the society is possible only through the perfection and spiritual transfiguration of the separate individual units.

Aurobindo thinks that since both the individual and the society are manifestations of the divine reality there should not be any antagonism in their aims and practice. A balance has to be arrived at, and the ideal law of social development is the rule of perfect individuality and perfect reciprocity—self-realisation is the sense, secret or covert, of individual and of social development. Aurobindo and Tagore think that society is organic and has a soul or is a soul, but the individual also is a spiritual self. We find emphasis both on the organic concept of the social totality and the spiritual-cosmic character of the individual. The key political concept of Aurobindo's political philosophy is reciprocity and mutuality between the individual and the society.

According to Aurobindo, increasing rational organisation, planning and conscious ordering are the characteristics of the modern social structures. The community, like the society, is also *spiritual* in its ultimate basis but unlike the case with society he does not refer to its vital basis. He said, "The spiritual mind of India regarded life as a manifestation of the self: the community was the body of the creator *Brahma*, the people was a life body of *Brahma* in the *samasti*, the collectivity, it was the collective *Narayana*, the individual was *Brahma* in the *vyasti*, the separate *jiva*, the individual *Narayana;* the king was the living representative of the Divine and the other orders of the community the natural powers of the collective self, *Prakritayah*."[6]

Aurobindo accepts the idea of the soul-manifestation of the collectivity. To him, the spirit is immortal, and the cultivation of spiritual powers can lead to a constant prolongation of collective life and historical existence. He said, "The idea is itself only the principle of soul manifestation of the communal being and each communal soul again a manifestation and vehicle of the greater eternal spirit that expresses itself in time and on earth is seeking, as it were, its own fullness in humanity through the vicissitudes of the *human cycle*"[7]. The concept of the spiritual dynamic in history differentiates his political philosophy from that of Hegel. He and Hegel accept the manifestation and revelation of the cosmic spirit in history. He has a far greater belief in the cosmic historical powers of the spirit which can make possible the evergrowing progression of the same people or nation.

Aurobindo always emphasises the spiritual importance of the individual. He said, "The individual as spirit or being is not confined within his humanity; he has been less than human, he can become more than human. The universe finds itself through him even as he finds himself in the universe, but he is capable of becoming more than the universe, since he can surpass it and enter into something in himself and in it and beyond it that is absolute. He is not confined within the community; although his mind and life are, in a way, part of the communal mind and life, there is something in him that can go beyond them. The community exists by the individual, for its mind and life and body are constituted by the mind and life and body of its comprising individuals; if that were abolished or disaggregated, its own existence would be abolished or disaggregated, though some spirit or power of it might form again in other individuals; but the *individual* is not a mere cell of the collective existence; he would not cease to exist if separated or expelled from the collective mass. For the collectivity, the community is not even the whole of humanity and it is not the world: the individual can exist and find himself elsewhere in humanity or by himself in the world. If the community has a life dominating that of the individuals which constitute it, still it does not constitute their whole life. If it has its being which it seeks to affirm by the life of the individuals, the individual also has a being of his own which he seeks to affirm in the life of the *community*. But he is not tied to that, he can affirm himself in another communal life, or, if he is strong enough, in a nomad existence or in an eremite solitude where, if he cannot pursue or achieve a complete material living, he can spiritually exist and find his own reality and indwelling self of being".[8]

Aurobindo differentiates between the soul of the community and communal *egoism*. To him, the ego is only an external false substitute for the central psychic being—the *Caitya Purusha*. It is a force of division, separation and limitation. It is only a subordinate and superficial formulation of the self-consciousness and self-experience of the subliminal self. The descent of overmental power would lead to the final abolition of the ego. But just as the *ego* operates on the individual level it can also operate on the national and communal level, and so instead of concord and mutual harmonious reciprocity we get constant struggles between collective egos. He said, "The communal ego, this obscure collective being, is not the soul or self of the community, it is a life-force that rises from the subconscient and , if denied the light of guidance by the reason, can be driven only by dark massive forces which are powerful but dangerous for the race".[9]

Aurobindo's philosophy of the state is related to his theory of the role of *reason* in the socio-political evolution of man. The first stage of human evolution is infra-rational and is marked by the dominance of instincts, haphazard institutions and impulses. The second stage is the rational age when the communal mind becomes more and more intellectually self-conscious. The third stage belongs to the future and would be marked by greater stress on the suprarational subjective consciousness. The state represents the great instrument of transition from the first stage to the second stage. He said, "The state is the masterful but arbitrary and intolerant science and reason of man that successfully takes the place of the intuitions and evolutionary experimentations of Nature, intelligent organisation replaces natural organism".[10]

The history of the state represents an advancing process of political unification and solidification through the development of a central focus of organised power. The state is based on territorial centralisation which leads to legislative and administrative *centralisation*. In other words, the state is synchronistic with the centralisation of political power. The rational and mechanically organised state marks the growth of organised legal order represented through the structure of an impersonal bureaucratic mechanism. It leads to the growth of order, efficiency, rigidity and uniformity. He said, "The intelligent will of the whole society expressed in carefully thought-out law and ordered regulation replaces its natural organic will expressed in a mass of customs and institutions which have grown up as the result of its nature and temperament. In the last perfection of the state, a carefully devised, in the end a giant machinery, productive and regulative, replaces the vigour and fertility of life with the natural simplicity of its great lines and the obscure, confused, luxuriant complexity of its details".[11]

Aurobindo is against the attribution of any ethical or moral character to the state. He said, "It has no soul or only a rudimentary one. It is a military, political and economic force; but it is only in a slight and undeveloped degree, if at all, an intellectual and ethical being. And unfortunately the chief use it makes of its undeveloped intellect is to blunt by fictions, catchwords and recently by state philosophies, its ill-developed ethical conscience".[12]

The organised state is not the representative of the best mind and best idealism of a nation. Often the state comes to be a collective *egoism* much interior to the best of which the *community* is capable. Aurobindo thinks that the attempt of the state to grow into an intellectual and moral being is a very interesting phenomenon of the modern world. He said, "But the claim of the state to absorb all free individual activities, a claim which it increasingly makes as it grows more clearly conscious of its new ideals and possibilities, is, to say the least of it, premature and, if satisfied, will surely end in a check to human progress, a comfortably organised stagnancy such as overtook the Graeco-Roman world after the establishment of the Roman Empire".[13]

Aurobindo repudiates the organic conception of the *state*. He said, "The state is bound to act crudely and in the mass; it is capable of that free, harmonious and intelligently or instinctively varied action which is proper to organic growth. For the state is not an organism, it is a machinery, and it works like a machine, without tact, taste, delicacy or intuition. It tries to manufacture, but what humanity is here to do is to grow and create".[14] The purpose of education is to create a developed personality by fostering inward growth of a man's faculties and powers. But a state-controlled education amounts to indoctrination and the spread of propaganda for creeds and cults dear to the party in actual power.

According to Aurobindo, "the business of the state is to remove obstacles, to remove all really harmful waste and friction. . . . and removing avoidable injustice, to secure for every individual a just and equal chance of self-development and satisfaction to the extent of his powers and in the line of his nature. . . . But all unnecessary interference with the freedom of man's growth is or can be harmful".[15] Hence he thinks that although it is possible to have a national education, a national religion and a national culture, a state *education*, a state culture or a state *religion* represent an absurd monstrosity and an unnecessary accentuation of the power of the state. To him, the goal of the individual is the attainment of gnostic consciousness and spiritual salvation, the state is at best, a machine to realise the socialist social and economic ideal.

In Aurobindo's view, the spiritually free *individual* does not owe his final obligation to the social and ethical institutions but to the spiritual being within him. He is hostile to the state and favours the nation. Both Hegel and Aurobindo accept the rational nature of the state but their conception of reason in a social perspective is fundamentally different. Aurobindo says that the state symbolises the transition from the impulsive, intuitional and instinctive ways of social experimentation to a rational order but evidently he means here, by reason, the subjective, discursive and analytic reason of individuals and groups. He thinks that the state is always to be conceived of as a means and never as an end.

Aurobindo's conception of the *state* is also different from that of the Oxford Idealists. To him, the social institutions have an intrinsic immanent importance and do not depend for their significance on the political order. He does not attribute the philosophic supremacy to art. He would also like to transcend ultimately even the absolutism of the religious and philosophic consciousness in the integral spiritual cosmic-transcendental consciousness. He believes that the *individual* contains the central spiritual value. We find a synthesis of spiritual idealism and the political importance of the individual in him. Individual rights are not derived from the state but originate in the psychological and sociological structure and situation of man. He identified the mind of the community with the totality of individual minds.

Aurobindo was reacting against the dominance of Vedantic illusionism, Buddhist idealism and Madhyamika nihilism and his problem was to emphasise the positive aspects of the *Vedanta* as a gospel of life and world-fulfilment. Besides being a *yogi* and a *mystic* seer he has constructed a political philosophy on the basis of the insight of the *Vedanta* and some kindred patterns in Western thought. But his hostility to the state is fundamental. He can never conceive of the state as a divine movement on earth or as a realised moral substance. He is significant because he exalts the moral and spiritual worth of the individual.

Aurobindo has significant anarchist elements in his thought. He is happy at the prospect of a spiritualised anarchism. *Anarchism* condemns the mechanisation, exaggerated regimentation and authoritarianism of the modern state. In the place of constraint anarchism stresses voluntary and spontaneous cooperation. Anarchism regards the state as an engine of exploitation. Anarchism believes in the fundamental goodness of human nature. It advocates a moral and even a political revolution to destroy the state.

Aurobindo distinguishes between the three schools of anarchism. The vitalistic or violent form of anarchism deliberately protests against any formal principle of organisation and claims the right of man to live his own life. He is opposed to this form of anarchism. He recognises the great services rendered by social regulation and organisation in the evolution of man. He believes it to be possible that the external legal and political mechanism may be replaced by an inner law and a code of self-imposed obligations. To him, intellectual anarchism has two psychological foundations. First, it recognises that the human mind which claims liberty for itself will be ready to guarantee the right of others to an equal amount of freedom. Secondly, it emphasises the existence of a natural sympathy and fellow-feeling in man and regards it possible to construct a social and political system founded on freedom, equality and spontaneous cooperation on the basis of the altruistic psychological substructure.

Intellectual anarchism operates with a higher and nobler concept of the nature of man than violent anarchism. Aurobindo said, "But there is a higher, an intellectual anarchist thought which in its aim and formula recovers and carries to its furthest logical conclusions a very real truth of nature and of the divine in man. In its revolt against the opposite exaggeration of the social principle, we find it declaring that all government of man by man by the power of compulsion is an evil, a violation, a suppression or a deformation of a natural principle of good which would otherwise grow and prevail for the perfection of the human race. Even the social principle in itself is questioned and held liable for a sort of fall in man from a natural to an unnatural and artificial principle of living".[16]

At an ultimate level, Aurobindo wants the realisation of the vision of an spiritual society. He wants that the spiritual sources of inner governance should become the guide for human existence. He said, "As it expresses itself at the present day, there is much in it that is exaggerated and imperfect. Its seers seem often to preach an impossible self-abnegation of the vital life and an *asceticism* which instead of purifying and transforming the vital being, seeks to suppress and even kill it, life itself is impoverished or dried up by this severe austerity in its very springs. Carried away by a high-reaching spirit of revolt, these prophets denounce civilisation as a failure because of its vitalistic exaggerations, but set up an opposite exaggeration which might well cure civilisation of some of its crying faults and ugliness, but would deprive it also of many real and valuable gains".[17]

Aurobindo thinks that some of the advocates of spiritual anarchism lay great emphasis on *asceticism* and *self-abnegation*. He believes that the prime condition for a better future is to bring to the surface the hidden powers of the spirit. He wants the motive-force for the ideal society to be a sense of spiritual comradeship, which means the realisation of an inner union. The spiritual anarchism as visualised by him would be realised in a perfectly spiritualised society. He thinks that even if the attainment of the ideal spiritual or spiritualised anarchism may appear to be a distant and far off consumption, perhaps the realisation of the ideal of philosophic anarchism may not be so remote. He would plead for the final realisation of the essence of spiritualised anarchism in a spiritualised society.

Aurobindo does not want *anarchism* harmfully to affect the benefits of *civilisation* and culture. He thinks that the principal defect of anarchist political philosophy is that it contemplates the elimination of the state before the deep social force of human brotherhood has become a realised social category. The central theme of his political philosophy is not to inculcate spiritual anarchism. His main emphasis is on the spiritualisation of human life. His aim is not to launch a crusade against the present mechanisms and organs of social and political order. His aim is to enunciate the progressive incorporation of the spiritual element in collective life.

Aurobindo is critical of modern institutional devices like *socialism* and *democracy* to solve the problems of society and politics. He does acknowledge that both democracy and socialism are products of the self-conscious evolution of society. He said, "In the process of its evolution from an infra-rational, instinctive natural stage, society attempts to perfect consciously by means of the state the whole organisation of its life, military, political, administrative, economic, social, cultural. The completeness of the process depends on the completeness of development by which the state and society become, as far as that may be, synonymous. That is the importance of democracy; that is the importance of socialism. They are the sign that the society is getting ready to be an entirely self-conscious and therefore a freely and consciously self-regulating organism".[18] He does not think that the institutionalised patterns of modern democracy and socialism represent the highest consummation of social rationality.

According to Aurobindo, there are two foundational principles of individualistic *democracy*. First, all individuals are to have equal political say, not because their actual equality is empirically demonstrable but because otherwise there would be the dominance of a socially and economically powerful segment in society. Secondly, it is morally sound that as long as an individual does not encroach upon the rights of others he should be allowed to govern his life according to the dictates of his own reason. *Democracy*, believes that mass education and political freedom can solve most of the problems that confront man. He distinguishes the mentality and political orientations of the aristocratic and monarchical states from democracies which are bourgeois states in the form either of a constitutional monarchy or a middle-class republic.

Democracy is interpreted in two ways. First it signifies a political institutional mechanism through which the citizens of a country can register their political will on basic social and political issues. This is an interpretation of democracy in the purely political sense. Secondly, democracy is regarded as a philosophy of life denoting a humane and equalitarian orientation. Aurobindo considers the democratic political form to be a contribution of Western civilisation. He analyses the principal political ideas behind Greek democracy. He thinks that an effective share in the governmental process by each citizen and a great freedom of individual action and temperament were the two main ideas behind Greek democracy. To him, a certain democracy equality is inevitable in a small community. Democracy, socialism and pacifism are to a great extent the by-products of, or at least vitally inspired by, the inward presence of the idea of humanism.

Aurobindo thinks there have been four consequences of the individualistic democratic ideal in practice. First, although the concept of the equality has been loudly preached, in actual practice a dominant class has obtained social and political leadership in the name of democracy. The second consequence of individualistic democracy has been an increasing effort on the part of the exploited and the under-privileged to assert their rights. There is the possibility of a war of classes. Thirdly, there is a perpetual strife of parties as a logical result of this class struggle. Fourthly, there is a growing stress of competition which replaces the ordered tyrannies of the infra-rational periods of humanity by a sort of ordered conflict. And this conflict ends in the survival not of the spiritually, rationally or physically fittest, but of the most fortunate and vitally successful.

Aurobindo criticises *democracy* on various grounds. First, the "mass consciousness by itself moves by a vague, half-formed or unformed subliminal and commonly subconscient impulse rising to the surface; it is prone to a blind or half-seeing unanimity which suppresses the individual in the common movement: if it thinks, it is by the motto, the slogan, the watch-word, the common crude or formed idea, the traditional, the accepted customary notion; it acts, when not by instinct or an impulse, then by the rule of the pack, the herd mentality, the type law".[19] He is opposed to the governance of the democratic cultus of the average man. The second criticism against democracy is that virtually it amounts not to the government of the people by and for the people, but to the rule of the bourgeoise and the ascendency of the plutocratic sections. He thinks that perfect and real democracy exists nowhere in the world and everywhere the propertied and professional classes and the bourgeoisie governed in the name of the people.

The trend towards the growth of an elite is the third criticism against *democracy*. Whatever the external form, real governance is by a small group. Aurobindo said, "The society has no discoverable common reason and will belonging alike to all its members; for the group-soul rather works out its tendencies by a diversity of opinions, a diversity of wills, a diversity of life, and the vitality of the group-life depends largely upon the working of this diversity, its continuity, its richness. Since that is so, government by the organised state must mean always government by a number of individuals—whether that number be in theory the minority or the majority makes in the end little fundamental difference. For even when it is the majority that nominally governs, it is in fact always the reason and will of a comparatively few effective men—and not really any common reason and will of all—that rules and regulates things with the consent of the half-hypnotised mass".[20]

Fourthly, Aurobindo is critical of the mechanism of modern representative *democracy*. His criticism amounts to the statement of the empirical fact that the legislators do not really represent the electorate. He said, "In large states, the personal share of each citizen in the government cannot be effective; he can only have an equal share—illusory for the individual although effective in the mass—in the periodical choice of his legislators and administrators. Even if these have not practically to be elected from a class which is not the whole or even the majority of the community, at present almost everywhere the middle class, still these legislators and administrators do not really represent their electors. The power they represent is another, a formless and bodiless entity, which has taken the place of monarch and aristocracy, that impersonal group-being which assumes some sort of outward form and body and conscious action in the huge mechanism of the modern state. Against this power, the individual is much more helpless than he was against old oppressions".[21] He is justified in pointing out the growing insignificance of the individual in the complex mechanism of the modern industrial society and bureaucratic administrative order.

Aurobindo is correct in emphasising the danger to *liberty* from democratic majority rule. He said, "But there is a deprivation of liberty which is more respectable in appearance, more subtle and systematised, more mild in its method because it has a greater force at its back, but for that very reason more effective and pervading. The tyranny of the majority has become a familiar phrase and its deadening effects have been depicted with a great force of resentment by a few of the modern intellectuals; but what the future promises us is something more formidable still, the tyranny of the whole, of the self-hypnotised mass over its constituent groups and units".[22] He refers to the chances of mass *hypnotism* and fury leading to the suppression of the intermediate associations and groups. He is a strong advocate of the revival and revitalisation of group life and he would definitely refuse to adhere to Rousseau's conception that the growth of intermediate associates interposes particular wills and raises impediments in the path of the concretisation of the general will.

Democracy advocates the techniques of compromise, persuasion, negotiation, bargaining and concessions; it cannot satisfy the fanatic of any cult. It will not satisfy the anarchist who revolts against the least idea of governmental and social constraint. Aurobindo said, "It is not likely that the immediate future of the democratic tendency will satisfy the utmost dreams of the lover of liberty who seeks an *anarchist* freedom, or of the lover of equality who tries to establish a socialistic dead level, or of the lover of fraternity who dreams of a world embracing communism".[23] Trial and error are necessary for the growth of the moral personality of a man or a group. By repeated experiments people will learn how to govern themselves. He would not agree that a democracy having destroyed the evils associated with majority rule and party government would be the last stage of social evolution, as is suggested in some quarters.

Aurobindo is opposed to the Benthamite *utilitarianism* as an ethical and political norm. Bentham supported free trade, low taxation, the abolition of intermediate economic associations and unfettered competition. Politically, the Benthamites stood for democratic *republicanism* and an ordered system of law. Aurobindo criticises Benthamism from the standpoint of idealistic ethics. He said, "Its shallow portentous errors, its substitution of a practical, outward and occasional test for the inner, subjective and absolute motive of ethics, its reduction of ethical action to an impossibly scientific and quite impracticable jugglery of moral mathematics, attractive enough to the reasoning and logical mind, quite false and alien to the whole instinct and intuition of the ethical being".[24]

For Aurobindo the true criterion of ethical action lies in the perception and realisation of the sense of good which exists in man almost by instinct. From the standpoint of moral conduct in the empirical world, he is opposed to the mere calculation of personal gain and loss and wants the enshrinement and the pursuit of the good of others and most widely the good of all. He pleads that man should stick to his principle of good, his instinct for good, his vision of good, his intention of good and to govern by that his conduct. He said, "It has been felt and said that the laws of right, the laws of perfect conduct are the laws of the gods, eternal beyond, laws that man is conscious of and summoned to obey. . . . If man's conscience is a creation of his evolving nature, if his conceptions of ethical law are mutable and depend on his stage of evolution, yet at the root of them there is something constant in all their mutations which lies at the very root of his own nature and of world-nature. . . . Below hides that secret of good in all things which the human being approaches and tries to deliver partially through ethical instinct and ethical idea; above is hidden the eternal good which exceeds our partial and fragmentary ethical conceptions".[25] He attacks utilitarianism from the idealistic standpoint. His emphasis is on the spiritual perfection of the human being.

Aurobindo is opposed to the capitalist system of economy. He is alarmed at the growth of capitalist concentrations because they accentuate the exploitationist power and strength of the capitalists. He said, "In commerce also so long as we follow the European spirit and European model, the individual competitive selfishness, the bond of mere interest in the joint-stock company or that worst and most dangerous development of cooperative capitalism, the giant octopus—like trust and syndicate, we shall never succeed in rebuilding a healthy industrial life".[26] He criticised the economic polity of England in India. He said, "The huge price India has to pay England for the inestimable privilege of being ruled by Englishmen is a small thing compared with the murderous drain by which we purchase the more exquisite privilege of being exploited by British capital".[27]

Aurobindo prophesied the collapse of *capitalism* after the First World War. He thought that capitalism had lost its moral force. He said, "The existing European system of civilisation at least in its figure of capitalistic industrialism has reached its own monstrous limits, broken itself by its own mass and is condemned to perish".[28] He does not advocate violent insurrection or organised proletarian revolution to bring that consummation about. He does not believe that the fall of capitalism is inevitable. It is possible that the world may remain divided between capitalists and communists. He is inspired by the socialist ideal of providing a simply rich and beautiful life for all. He remains a critic both of socialism and capitalism.

According to Aurobindo, the Darwinian-Spencerian formula of evolution led to the evolution of the concept of a social organism and this concept helped the development of economic socialism. To him, socialism has been considerably influenced by individualism. *Individualism* professes two aims of thought and action. First, it wants a universalised canons of objective truth for testing human judgements. Secondly, it wants a generalised norm as a pattern for the organisation of the social being. He said, "In seeking the truth and law of his own being the individual seems to have discovered a truth and law which is not of his own individual being at all, but of the collectively, the pack, the hive, the mass. The result to which this points and to which it still seems irresistibly to be driving us is a new ordering of society by a rigid economic or governmental socialism".[29]

Socialism aims at an equitable distribution of the wealth of the society, or else would like to concentrate wealth in the hands of the state. Aurobindo said, "The society, still more than the family, is essentially economic in its aims and in its very nature. That accounts for the predominantly economic and materialistic character of modern ideas of socialism, for these ideas are the full rationalistic flowering of this instinct of collective life".[30] To him, *socialism* is an extension of the nationalist idea. He said, "Socialism is really an attempt to complete the growth of the national community by making the individual do what he has never yet done, live for the community more than for himself. It is an outgrowth of the national, not of the international idea".[31] It is possible to demonstrate the empirical and historical connection between socialism and the national idea. To him, socialism has been international and pacific because of the conditions of its birth. War is favourable to the rule of the upper classes and is used in their interests, while the classes whose interests socialism claims to represent do not hope to gain by war.

According to Aurobindo, "German socialism, the protagonist of the idea of massively leading the way in this formidable abjuration. It is true that a small minority in each country either remained heroically faithful to its principles or soon returned to them. . . . Russian socialism, it may be said, has at least in its extremer form, shown a stronger root of internationalistic feeling. But what it has actually attempted to accomplish is a development of labour rule on the basis of a purified nationalism, non-aggressive except for revolutionary purposes and self-contained, and not on the larger international idea".[32] He refers to the role of the intellectuals in the development and spread of the socialist ideology and movement. To him, socialism and *syndicalism* have been a revolt of labour aided by a number of intellectuals against the established state of things.

Socialism does not mean the substitution of the power of the bourgeois state by a spontaneously cooperative non-coercive social syndicate to Aurobindo. It amounts to the full efflorescence and concretisation of state power. He said, "The state principle leads necessarily to uniformity, regulation, mechanisation, its inevitable and is socialism. There is nothing fortuitous, no room for chance in political and social development, and the emergence of socialism was no accident or a thing that might not have been, but the inevitable result contained in the very seed of the state idea.[33] He is intensely attracted by the social and economic egalitarianism of socialism while at the same time he has a great horror of socialist *authoritarianism*. He thinks that state control and direction are the essence of socialism. Socialism represents the omni competence of the all-jealous state and, therefore, to him, totalitarianism is the natural, almost inevitable destiny of socialism.

Aurobindo is apprehensive of the extension of state power under socialism. He is a critic of socialist centralisation and authoritarianism. Socialism considers the state to be a means for the collective operation of the resources of the society. He is a critic of the increasing dominance of the state under socialism. *Socialism* contemplates the elimination of class exploitation and economic competition and the extablishment of an all-coordinating governance and organisation of socio-economic life by the state. According to Aurobindo in the Scandinavian countries a temporising, reformist practical socialism compromising between the right regulation of the communal life and the freedom of the individual has to some extent made good.

Modern socialism is not equivalent to economic equalitarianism. Aurobindo said, "To eliminate poverty, not by the crude idea of equal distribution but by the holding of all property in common and its management by the organised state, to equalise opportunity and capacity as far as possible through universal education and training, again by means of the organised state, is the fundamental idea of modern *socialism*".[34] Socialisation of the means of production is bound to lead to the growth of the power of the state. To him, totalitarianism, whether it be practised by fascism or communism, spells repression, savagery and tyranny and he is vigorously opposed to that.

According to Aurobindo the ideal of the perfectly organised state is socialistic. He said, "In Russia the Marxist system of socialism has been turned almost into a gospel. Originally a rationalistic system worked out by a logical thinker and discoverer and systematiser of ideas, it has been transformed by the peculiar turn of the Russian mind into something like a social religion, a collectivist mystique, an inviolable body of doctrines with all denial or departure treated as a punishable heresy, a social cult enforced by the intolerant piety and enthusiasm of a converted people".[35] He is critical of the hesitating and vacillating character of social democracy which at times led to the rise of totalitarianism and dictatorship in several countries.

Aurobindo envisages that at some future time *socialism* might possibly become even imperialistic. He said, "And if socialism triumphs in the leading nations of the world, it will inevitably seek to impose its rule everywhere not only by indirect pressure, but even by direct intervention in what it could consider backward countries".[36] He is also critical of modern fascism. He said, "The connection between socialism and the democratic or equalitarian idea or the revolt of the proletariat is, however, an accident of history, not its essence. In Italian *fascism* there arose a socialism undemocratic and non-equalitarian in its form, idea and temper".[37]

Aurobindo thought that a possible tussle between *capitalism* and *communism* might occur. He is aware of the bipolarisation of the world political structure after the Second World War. Referring to the expansionist urge in communism, he said, "It now seems probable that the future will belong to a struggle between communism and a surviving Capitalistic Industrialism in the New World or even between communism and a more moderate system of social democracy in the two continents of the Old World".[38] But he thinks that a final Armageddon between communism and capitalism is not inevitable. He does not adhere to that kind of destructive determinism. He visualises the possibility of a reproachment although in some of his earlier writings he also accepted the inevitability of a future duel between socialism and bourgeois-democracy.

Aurobindo does not believe that *communism* is committed to a nihilistic destruction of existing world civilisation, as it is misrepresented by some of its rabid opponents. He does not believe that socialism would become generally prevalent in the world. It is significant from the standpoint of Asian politics that the ideal of the social and economic betterment of the people, as formulated by socialism, has greatly appealed to him. He appreciates the economic philosophy of socialism because it promises a rich and aesthetically cultivated life for all, but is intensely critical of the political techniques of organised socialist absolutism.

Aurobindo would plead for a deeper sentiment of fraternity as the real social bond. He thinks that the socialists are mistaken in attempting to build a regime of *equality* in the absence of spiritual fraternity. He visualises the dawn of the spiritual comradeship which is the expression of an inner realisation of oneness. For so only can egoism disappear and the true individualism of the unique godhead in each man found itself on the true communism of the equal godhead in the race. He is hostile to the modern political and economic formulas devised by Western Political thinkers.

In the early days Aurobindo was struggling for the emancipation of his countrymen from an alien regime. He was fighting for political and economic *freedom*. In his later days he was fighting on a spiritual plane for the descent of supramental power for the moral and spiritual freedom of humanity from the forces of darkness and inconscience. The spiritual problem for man is the quest for divine perfection and immortality, which means the establishment of an infinite freedom in place of mechanical necessity. He does not accept the theory that cosmic phenomena proceed from the mechanical inevitability of a non-rational natural necessity, but believes in the teleological involution and evolution in the world of the transcendent-universal spiritual absolute.

Aurobindo says that absolute freedom, even when within the bounds of the mortal frame, can be won if one makes a voluntary self-surrender to the supreme spirit and becomes an agent for the effectuation of the works of the divine. To him, the conquest of necessity is not effectuated by an intelligent cognition of the processes of material forces and the socio-economic reality as is, stressed by modern science, but is a result of spiritual realisation and a dynamic integral transmutation of the human consciousness.

Self-realisation means the ever-present consciousness of the eternal freedom of the spirit. Aurobindo said, "Spirituality respects the freedom of the human soul, because it is in itself fulfilled by freedom; and the deepest meaning of freedom is to expand and grow towards perfection by the law of one's own nature, *Dharma*".[39] Spiritual freedom does not mean the assertion of the exaggerated claims of the vital ego, but it means obedience to the Divine Truth in ourselves and our members and in all around us. The concept of spiritual freedom or *self-realisation* implies the positive expansion and extension of the ordinary consciousness. This implies obedience to the laws of our spiritual being. His idea of freedom as obedience to the laws of our spiritual being postulates the growth of a communal fraternity and even of the accentuation of human feelings of sympathy, fellowship and kindness, because obedience to the laws of our being implies a unity without limits for that is our real being.

According to Aurobindo, "The *liberty* claimed by the struggling human mind for the individual is no mere egoistic challenge and revolt, however egoistically or with one-sided exaggeration and misapplication it may sometimes be advanced; it is the divine instinct within him, the law of the self, its claim to have room, and the one primary condition for its natural self-unfolding".[40] The consummation of *freedom*, which is planted in man as a divine instinct, implies the deliverance from the animal elements and the progressive and deepening inward growth into spirituality. Freedom is an essential attribute of the soul and not of the objectified material nature and where there is no soul there can be no freedom. The conception of the freedom of the spirit, postulated by him, is not the mere reiteration of the gospel of redemption from the sins and sorrows of the world as popularised in ancient religions and philosophies.

Aurobindo has developed the concept of *spiritual freedom*. He says that the ideas of internal and spiritual freedom has been developed in the East, while the idea of social and political freedom is a legacy of the Western civilisation. He points out that in Europe the ideal of external freedom is important, whereas in India the theory of inner freedom has been stressed. He said, "They (the Europeans) have found out the way to *external freedom*. We have found out the way to *internal freedom*. We meet and give to each other what we have gained. We have learned from them to aspire after external as they will learn from us to aspire after internal freedom".[41] He is not unmindful of the significance of the sentiments of *fraternity*, fellow-feeling and equality as expressed in Christianity, Islam and Hinduism, but he said, "Still we learned from them (the Europeans) to strive after political equality and in return for what they have given us we shall lead them to the secret of the equality within".[42]

According to Aurobindo, *Swaraj* is the organisation of national self-help and national self-dependence but it is more than a mere organisation of the independent life of the country into centres of strength which grow out of its conditions and answer to its needs, so as to make a single and organic whole. The perfect human order can be realised not by imperfect unregenerate individuals but only by the collective efforts of individuals who have realised inner freedom or moral *Swaraj*. Only a spiritual supra-rational enlightenment can bring perfect order and harmony in the world. He thinks that inner freedom will also lead to material and political success. He holds that inner freedom leads to outer freedom. He said, "The first thing that a nation must do is to realise the true freedom that is within us and it is only when you understand that free within is free without, you will be really free. It is for this reason that we preach the gospel of unqualified *Swaraj*".[43]

Aurobindo is thoroughly convinced that *spirituality* will bring the fullness to man's seeking for political and social perfection and to all his other powers and aspirations. During his days as a prophet of nationalism he exhorted his countrymen to win back this inner *Swaraj* before the outer kingdom could be conquered. He pleads for both inner and outer freedom. He wants that the freedom of man within as well as without should be vindicated. *Inner freedom* is necessary for individuals because it leads to the acquisition of divine power, therefore he formulated his conception of inner *Swaraj*. He would not be satisfied only with inner freedom. He pleads for the synthesis of outer and inner freedom.

For Aurobindo the individual is a formation of the *spirit*. he regards the society and the community also as formations of the spiritual reality. But he thinks that since the collectivity can obtain perfection only through individuals, the *individual* is the key to the evolutionary movement. The individual always remains the focal point in the political and spiritual philosophy of Aurobindo. Rights are necessary for the realisation of individual perfection. Rights are those principles which make the objectivisation of the processes and means of individual self-development and collective perfection possible. To him, rights are claimed for the full development of the individual and society. He accepts that the individual has *rights* against the state.

Aurobindo points out that the suppression of the individual is a danger to social and political advancement. The conscious growth of the individual towards progressive enlightenment is a more readily accomplishable possibility than the education of the mass because the latter is still obscure, half-conscious, ruled by universal forces that escape its mastery and its knowledge. Under the influence of ancient Indian political and metaphysical thought he formulates the ideal of spiritual individualism. The spiritual *individualism* leads to the formulation of the philosophy of eventual transcendence of social and political obligations. He said, "The individual does not owe his ultimate allegiance either to the state which is a machine or to the community which is a part of life and not the whole of life: his allegiance must be to the Truth, the self, the spirit, the Divine which is in him and in all; not to subordinate, or lose himself in the mass, but to find and express that truth of being in himself and help the community and humanity in its seeking for its own truth and fullness of being must be the real object of existence".[44]

By stressing the theory of the transcendence of social and political claims Aurobindo pleads for a spiritual *anarchism*. But he will never plead for the transcendence of social and political obligations by any and every empirical individual. The transcendence of socio-political claims is dependent upon the proportionate to the development of spiritual consciousness. *Spiritual freedom* does not imply a life entirely separate from cosmic and social existence. It leads to the growth of a sense of spiritual oneness and solidarity with all living beings. The spiritual awareness leading to spiritual oneness harmonises the claims of true individualism and true collectivism in the integral consciousness of the divine reality.

According to Aurobindo the claims of the *spirit* should have precedence over the claims of those collectivities that belong to the realm of the world. He considers that the state is only a machine and he will not agree with Othmar Spann that any assertion of the claims of individual liberty will lead to spiritual under-development. In his idealism, the individual is the becoming of the spirit and the transcendentally-oriented spiritual individual not only achieves an identification in inner consciousness with all living beings, their minds and feelings and aspirations, but sees them all as diverse and multiple becomings of the same reality. Such a person goes beyond the claims and persistent obligations of the community and the state. He stresses the great historical necessity of the social collectivity. He thoroughly emphasised the fulfilment of its claims and obligations by the spiritually unregenerate individuals.

Aurobindo never accepts the idea of the fulfilment of the demands of the *ego*. He is not an individualist in the sense of emphasising the self-sufficiency of the individual. He advocates an ethical doctrine beyond hedonism, sensationalism and utilitarianism. He preaches a subordination of sensuous living for the sake of spiritual realisation. He was a firm believer in religious *equality* and he believed that according to one's own inner make-up and psychological orientation one should progress in the religious path. He has always laid the emphasis on the spirit. He holds that the society also has a sub-soul. He holds that the community is a formation of the spiritual reality. He accepts the idea of harmony between the individual and the state for his ideal society.

According to Aurobindo, "The ideal society is characterised by a respect for individual liberty and free growth and a simultaneous respect for the needs, efficiency, solidarity, natural growth and organic perfection of the corporate being, the society or nation".[45] The threats to liberty arise from asserting the claims of the individual against those of his fellows. The spiritual society of the future will acknowledge the claims of *individual freedom*. He said, "A large liberty will be the law of a spiritual society and the increase of freedom a sign of the growth of human society towards the possibility of true spiritualisation".[46]

The important problem in politics is the reconcilisation of power and *liberty*. According to Aurobindo, "Perhaps liberty and equality, liberty and authority, liberty and organised efficiency can never be quite satisfactorily reconciled so long as man aggregates, lives by *egoism*, so long as he cannot undergo a great spiritual and psychological change and rise beyond mere communal association to . . . . the ideal of fraternity, or, less sentimentally and more truly expressed, an inner oneness. That no mechanism . . . . has ever created or can create, it must take birth in the soul and rise from hidden and divine depths within.[47] His solution for the perpetual conflict between power and liberty is a spiritual transformation of mankind.

Liberty and *equality* are difficult to harmonise at political level. Aurobindo said, "Freedom, equality and brotherhood are three godheads of the soul; they cannot be really achieved through the external machinery of society or by man so long as he lives only in the individual and the communal ego. When the ego claims liberty, it arrives at competitive individualism. When it asserts equality, it arrives first at strife, then at an attempt to ignore the variations of Nature, and as the sole way of doing that successfully, it constructs an artificial and machine-made society. A society that pursues liberty as its ideal is unable to achieve equality, a society that aims at equality will be obliged to sacrifice liberty".[48]

Aurobindo thinks that a purely political and institutional solution would not work. The solution of politics lies in metapolitics. He said, "The union of liberty and equality can only be achieved by the power of human brotherhood and it cannot be founded on anything else . . . . when the soul claims freedom, it is the freedom of its self—development, the self-development of the divine in man in all his being. When it claims equality, what it is claiming is that freedom equally for all and the recognition of the same soul, the same godhead in all human beings . . . . freedom, equality, and unity are the eternal attributes of the spirit".[49]

Aurobindo thinks the hidden power of the human soul has to be discovered for the real integration of freedom and equality. He would not deny the services of reason. He thinks that *socialism* and *democracy* represent the ideal of the conscious use of reason for social purposes. He would like mankind to proceed from the irrational stage of social action to the rational stage. He would not consider a highly rationalised society to be the climax of human perfection.

Aurobindo does not construct any new theory of law like Von Jhering, Kohler, Kelsen or Pound but he makes some observations on the problem of law with references to its bearings on liberty. He follows that realistic and sociological method in analysing the sources of the power of law. To him, there are two bases for the authority of law. First, the strong interest of the majority or of a dominant minority or the community as a whole in maintaining it. This view emphasises the sociological aspect of legal obedience. The second foundation of law is based on the monopolistic possession of the instruments of coercion by the law-enforcing agency. He minimises the importance of elements of rationality and universality involved in law, which impart to it an intrinsic force for commanding obedience.

Aurobindo distinguishes three stages in the evolution of *law*. First, the stage of unwritten or partly written system. Secondly, the stage represented by systematic institutes which, although they maintain the strict form of legal codification, are really only an ossification of custom and help to stereotype the life of the society and not to rationalise it. Thirdly, the stage of the deliberately ordered codes which are an attempt at intelligent legal systematisation. In this stage a sovereign authority establishes the law code. He pleads for the use of the legal mechanism for safeguarding liberty. he said, "Human society progresses really and vitally in proportion as law becomes the child of freedom, it will reach perfection when man having learned to know and become spiritually one with his fellow man, the spontaneous law of his society exists only as outward mould of his self-governed liberty".[50]

Aurobindo is never a positivist himself, like Austin. He said, "Better anarchy than the long continuance of a law which is not our own or which our real nature cannot assimilate. And all repressive or preventive law is only a makeshift, a substitute for the true law which must develop from within and be not a check on liberty, but its outward image and visible expression".[51] In the ultimate stage he wants the replacement of the coercive mechanism of law. He said, "The works of life right themselves, escape from confusion, substitute for the artificial or legal order imposed by the intellect and for the arbitrary rule of desire the guidance of the soul's inner insight, enter into the profound paths of the spirit".[52]

Freedom is a cardinal concept in idealistic political thought. The idea of making law the child and image of divine liberty, formulated by Aurobindo, shows the influence of Vedantic philosophy which emphasises that the basic goal of man is to transcend partial and egoistic standpoints and realise the spiritual being. His view of freedom as obedience to the laws of one's being is a reconciliation of the views of Rousseau and *Bhagavadgita*. Sometimes he defines freedom as obedience to divine laws and sometimes as obedience to the laws of one's being. He differentiates the ideas of *Sattvic* freedom and *Trigunatita* as found in the *Gita* from the stoic concept of freedom.

Both Aurobindo and Kant are agreed that the individual is to be treated not as a means but as an end. But in Aurobindo the emphasis in always on the cosmically-transcendentally-oriented spiritual individual, and not on the moral individual as in Kant. Both accept that there should be a universalistic motivation in human conduct. Aurobindo would go a step further than Kant and say that beyond the universal lies the transcendent and man has so to act as to achieve ultimate identity even with that supreme being. In Aurobindo inner freedom lies in obeying the law of God.

Aurobindo considers the state as only a machine and a contrivance. He holds that India has to teach Europe the conception of inner spiritual freedom. He believes that in the Vedanta there is a higher conception of spiritual freedom than in *Christianity*. He always pleads for a comprehensive conception of liberty. Even when he conceives of the society as an organism he always leaves room for stressing the supreme importance of the spiritual individual. He always upholds the unique spiritual essence of the individual. He thinks that progressive approximation to divine liberty amounts to the suppression of the demon in man and the growth into divine life. He has a far greater consciousness of the spiritual nature of the individual; he never preaches the complete political and social subordination of the individual either to the society or to the state. He advocates a comprehensive synthesis of external political freedom and inner moral and spiritual freedom.

Aurobindo emphasises the importance of the inner freedom of the human spirit. He has pleaded for a synthesis of external and internal freedom. He stresses the significance of the spiritual individual. He preaches the transcendence of political obligations and this amounts to advocating the subversion of the political structure. He regards the state as the product of reason. The growth of the state means the replacement of instinctive and infra-rational methods of social and political action by regularised and formalised techniques. The central point in his political philosophy is the conception of *freedom*. He has pleaded for a spiritual synthesis of liberty, equality, unity, peace and fraternity. He emphasises the necessity of spiritual metapolitics to solve the problems of politics.

REFERENCES

1. Sri Aurobindo, *The Human Cycle, op. cit.*, pp. 305-6.
2. Sri Aurobindo, *The Life Divine*, Vol. I, *op. cit.*, p. 18.
3. Sri Aurobindo, *The Ideal of Human Unity, op. cit.*, p. 84.
4. Sri Aurobindo, *The Human Cycle, op. cit.*, p. 41.
5. *Ibid.*, pp. 39-40.
6. Sri Aurobindo, *The Spirit and Form of Indian Polity, op. cit.*, p. 29.
7. *Ibid.*, pp. 19-20.
8. Sri Aurobindo, *The Life Divine*, Vol. II, pp. 920-21.
9. *Ibid.*, p. 929.
10. Sri Aurobindo, *Ideal of Human Unity, op. cit.*, p. 233.
11. *Ibid.*, pp. 232-33.
12. *Ibid.*, p. 24.

13. *Ibid.*, pp. 25-26.
14. *Ibid.*, p. 27.
15. *Ibid.*, p. 28.
16. Sri Aurobindo, *The Human Cycle, op. cit.*, p. 268.
17. *Ibid.*, pp. 272-73.
18. Sri Aurobindo, *The Ideal of Human Unity, op. cit.*, p. 211.
19. Sri Aurobindo, *The Life Divine*, Vol. II, p. 487.
20. Sri Aurobindo, *The Human Cycle, op. cit.*, p. 261.
21. Sri Aurobindo, *The Ideal of Human Unity, op. cit.*, pp. 291-92.
22. *Ibid.*
23. Sri Aurobindo, *The Ideal of the Karmayogin, op. cit.*, p. 39.
24. Sri Aurobindo, *The Human Cycle, op. cit.*, pp. 182-83.
25. *Ibid.*, pp. 186-87.
26. Sri Aurobindo, *The Ideal of the Karmayogin, op. cit.*, p. 27.
27. Sri Aurobindo, *The Doctrine of Passive Resistance, op. cit.*, p. 14.
28. Sri Aurobindo, *After the War, op. cit.*, p. 10.
29. Sri Aurobindo, *The Human Cycle, op. cit.*, pp. 21-22.
30. *Ibid.*, p. 200.
31. Sri Aurobindo, *The Ideal of Human Unity, op. cit.*, pp. 346-47.
32. *Ibid.*, p. 346.
33. *Ibid.*, pp. 286-87.
34. *Ibid.*, p. 84.
35. Sri Aurobindo, *The Human Cycle, op. cit.*, p. 255.
36. Sri Aurobindo, *The Ideal of Human Unity, op. cit.*, pp. 282-83.
37. *Ibid.*, pp. 265.
38. *Ibid.*, pp. 157.
39. Sri Aurobindo, *The Human Cycle, op. cit.*, p. 224.
40. *Ibid.*, pp. 80-81.
41. *Ibid.*, p. 273.
42. Sri Aurobindo, *Speeches, op. cit.*, p. 117.
43. *Ibid.*, p. 46.
44. Sri Aurobindo, *The Life Divine*, Vol. II, p. 921.
45. Sri Aurobindo, *The Ideal of Human Unity, op. cit.*, p. 146.
46. Sri Aurobindo, *The Human Cycle, op. cit.*, p. 283.
47. Sri Aurobindo, *The Ideal of Human Unity, op. cit.*, p. 130.
48. *Ibid.*, p. 368.
49. *Ibid.*, pp. 368-69.
50. *Ibid.*, p. 185.
51. *Ibid.*
52. Sri Aurobindo, *The Synthesis of Yoga*, Vol. I, *op. cit.*, p. 160.

4

AUROBINDO ON CIVILISATION AND CULTURE

Aurobindo repudiates the straightlinear theory of human progression. According to him there are periods of progression as well as of downward recoils, the whole constituting an *evolution* that is cyclic rather than in one straight line. He thinks it possible to have a theory not only of the cyclic evolution of social and political history, but also a universal theory of cycles of human evolution which is hinted at in the concept of the several *Manus* and *Manvantaras* in the *Puranas*. From the theory of cosmic progression is derived Aurobindo's view about the cyclical or spiral progression, or at least a very zig zag swinging curve of advance. A *cyclical theory* of historical evolution can be considered to have three significant characteristics. The theory of cosmic repetitions is also found in the *Puranas*.

Aurobindo derived the theory of the *human cycle* not only from the Vedanta, but has also been profoundly influenced by Karl Lamprecht. He said, "In pre-war Germany. . . . a first psychological theory of history was conceived and presented by an original intelligence. . . . A German historian, originator of this theory, seized on a luminous idea. . . . its basic idea formulated a suggestive and illuminating truth, and it is worthwhile following up some of the suggestions it opens out in the light especially of Eastern thought and experience".[1] Lamprecht divided German history into five stages. The first was the symbolic stage when in primitive Germany, fancy and imagination were dominant and the individual was almost merged in the family and the clan did not have any separate legal personality. In the second stage or the typal age of the Middle Ages, types were developed. The later Middle Ages saw the emergence of the third or conventional stage characterised by the territorial basis of political rule and the growth of urban centres. The *Renaissance* and the Reformation began the fourth stage, the age of individualism, which culminated in the Aufklarung and the rise of rationalistic philosophy. The Romantic movement with the reaction of Gefuhl against Verstand and Vernunft ushered in the fifth or the subjective stage. To him, history is not a purely psychic process but a socio-psychic process.

Although Aurobindo has been greatly influenced by Lamprecht, so much so that he writes a book covering over three hundred pages based on the conceptual scheme of the German historian, he still points out certain defects of the scheme. First, Lamprecht does not explain the inner meaning of the successive phases of historical evolution. Secondly, he does not demonstrate the logical necessity of the specific succession of the five phases. Thirdly, he does not discover the ultimate teleology towards which the historical process is moving. Aurobindo, on the other hand, firmly believes in the concept of a spiritual ultimate reality which manifests itself in history and thereby imparts an immanent meaning and a final *teleology* to the historic process.[2]

Aurobindo thinks that the Vedic Age represented the symbolic phase of Indian history, with *intuition*, mystic vision and imagination predominating. He has been possibly influenced by Dayananda. He has attempted the mystic interpretation of the Rigvedic hymns to *Agni*. To him, the Vedic *mystics* had four principal tenets. First, they represent a quest after the higher truth, a higher light and a discovery of the path to immortality. Secondly, they want to attain the Sun of gnostic truth, illumined knowledge and perfect right or *Rita*. Thirdly, they conceive of life in terms of a struggle between the forces of light, the *Devas*, and the forces of darkness, the *Asuras*; the constant aid of the gods is invoked for help and power. Fourthly, they believe in the ultimate reality of an ever conscient existence—the *Ekam Sat*.

Aurobindo thinks that *mystics* not only in India but also in other countries possessed the secrets of an esoteric science and were occultists. In the formulation of his own theory of spiritual law he has accepted the Vedic view of an immortal law and permanent truth, ever-active but operating differently according to the dynamic medium in which the work proceeds. He holds that the *Vedas* contain the secrets of an esoteric science now lost to the modern world. His *nationalism* becomes apparent in his statement that modern science is driving towards a monism which is consistent with multiplicity, and this he considers a drive towards the Vedic idea of the one essence with its many becomings.

The individualist stage of human society represents the age of protestantism, reason, revolt, progress and freedom. Aurobindo finds the seeds of *atheism, secularism* and *anarchism* in individualism, because the homo sapiens as a gigantic Prometheus is repelled by the authorities of God and state. He said, "The individualistic age of Europe was in its beginning a revolt of reason, in its culmination a triumphal progress of physical science".[3] He finds that the rationalistic individualistic *civilisation* of the West is spreading in the world because of the political rise and military triumph of European powers. He finds the rise of subjectivism in pre-war Germany, Ireland and India. He considers the appearance of the Bismarkian 'Blood and Iron' a misfortune for Germany in many respects "because his rude and powerful hand precipitated its subjectivity into form and action at too early a stage; a longer period of incubation might have produced results less disastrous to itself; if less violently stimulative to humanity".[4]

Aurobindo feels that there have been some gravely erroneous consequences of the false German subjectivism or the bastard creed of objective *subjectivism*. He interprets the First World War as a confused half struggle, half effort at accommodation between the old intellectual and materialistic and the new still superficial subjective and vitalistic impulses in the West. He thinks that the individualistic period in Asian history would neither be of long duration nor predominantly secularistic and intellectualistic. Due to its native subjectivism the East may evolve a new social dynamics based on spirituality and that may prove to be an important force in world politics.

According to Spengler every *culture* arises in the proto-soul of humanity. It has some fundamental prime symbols, for example, stone in the Egyptian culture, and pure and limitless space in the Faustian Western culture. Every culture in its last stage passes through a period of civilisation. Culture is characterised by spiritual creativeness and artistic and philosophical accomplishments while *internationalism, plutocracy, technology, urbanisation* and *materialism* characterise civilisation. Spengler thought that the Western peoples were passing through a period of civilisation. The basic difference between civilisation and culture is that the former looks to the outward, material, political and social accomplishments while culture is oriented towards artistic, ethical and spiritual excellence.

The term *culture* refers to the material artifacts as well as to the customs and institutions of the most primitive peoples. According to the anthropologists the term civilisation refers to the specialised and sophisticated aspects of the more advanced cultures. In his typological delineations of barbarism, civilisation and culture Aurobindo begins with his metaphysical assumptions about the successive emergence of matter, life and mind through evolutionary progression from the inconscient. He considers barbarism to be a savage state of complete immersion in a life of physical and material satisfactions.

According to Aurobindo, civilisations means the resplendence and flowering of vital sentiments and intellectual activities. It is an age of civil society, organised political and economic living and the growth of knowledge and science, but all these are used for the sake of maximisation of comforts, commodities and enjoyments. He criticised the *civilisation* on two grounds. First, its vitalistic engrossments are considered inadequate in the spiritualistic metaphysics of Aurobindo. Secondly, the excess of Western civilisation are condemned by him from the standpoint of an Indian nationalist.

According to Aurobindo, the characteristics of modern civilisation are *commercialism*, sensational vitalistic activism and a certain amount of *democratisation*. Commercialism is the fundamental sin of modern civilisation. The ancient period of human society was primarily religious and to some extent political. He is critical of the mechanical economics and the economic barbarism of the present age. The main characteristic of such an age is the quest after vital success, satisfaction, productiveness, accumulation, prossession, enjoyment, comfort and convenience for their own sake and not as intermediate agencies for a larger growth and fullness of being and existence.

In Aurobindo we find constant references to the dominance of selfishness, hatred, violence and the cult utility in Western civilisation. He refers more to the excesses of rationalism, vitalism and *philistinism* in Western civilisation. He takes a more dialectical and deterministic attitude. He thinks that even the mechanism, materialism, vitalism and rationalism of the West have been necessary instruments wielded by the Zeit-Geist to demonstrate the maximum possibilities of the physical and intellectual aspects of human life.

Aurobindo repudiates the cult of progress. The theory of progress is intimately connected with the concept of civilisation. He is critical of straightlinear theories of human progression. Being a moralist, he would try to replace the idea of purely material achievements by ethical growth and inward advance. Being a *spiritualist*, he would consider that only to be real progress which makes possible the advent of the spiritual age of the human cycle. To him, progress is an evolutionary ascent towards the acquisition of spiritual power, conscious awareness and delight. The mechanism of individual and social progress is a double movement of self-illumination of man and self-harmonisation with the intelligence and the intelligent will as the intermediaries between his soul and its works. His basic objection to the modern concept of progress is that it is too mechanical and it does not care to find out the basic teleology of social and economic progress.

Aurobindo seriously and emphatically challenges the foundations of the modern claim to progress and superiority. He said, "Man today is not wiser than the ancient seers and sages and thinkers—not more spiritual than the great seekers of old, the first mighty mystics, not superior in arts and crafts to the ancient artists and craftsmen; the old races that have disappeared showed as potent an intrinsic originality, invention, capacity of dealing with life; and, if modern man in this respect has gone a little further, not by any essential progress but in degree, scope, abundance, it is because he has inherited the achievements of his fore runners. Nothing warrants the idea that he will ever hew his way out of the half-knowledge, half-ignorance which is the stamp of its kind, or even if he develops a higher knowledge that he can break out of the outmost boundary of the mental circle".[5]

Aurobindo wants the development of culture. *Culture* signifies the pursuit of mental life for its own sake. The aim of a complete and integral culture is to raise and enlarge the internal man, the mind, the soul, the spirit on the basis of the social, political and economic foundations of a vitalistic civilisation. But as a specific concept culture is concerned with the total development of the mind. In the German concept of Kultur, according to Aurobindo, the emphasis was not merely on the acquisition of a set of intellectual generalisations but on the ordering and arrangement of life and society by ideas based on the truths of life. Aurobindo said, "It must be our definite verdict upon it that it was inferior as an age of culture to ancient Athens, to Italy of the Renascence, to ancient or classical India. For great as might be the deficiencies of social organisation in those eras and though their range of scientific knowledge and material achievement was immensely inferior, yet they were more advanced in the art of life, knew better its object, and aimed more powerfully at some clear ideal of human perfection".[6]

According to Aurobindo, there are four concepts which indicate the gradations in Greek ethical thought. First, the concept of Eupreps—that which is externally attractive and seemly. Secondly, Dikaion—that which is in accordance with justice or dike and convention or nomos. Thirdly, Agathon—the good which represents a combination both of the seemly and of the just. Fourthly, Kalon—the purely beautiful. He pleads for a synthesis of aesthetic and ethical cultures. He wants the synthesis of beauty and ethics to be attained by force of reason and will. He pleads for a harmonisation of ethics and beauty which are the respective manifestations of *Tapas* and *Ananda*. He said, "We can enlarge the sense of ethics by the sense of beauty and delight and introduce into it, to correct its tendency of hardness and austerity, the element of gentleness, love, amenity, the hedonistic side of morals; we can steady, guide and strengthen the delight of life by the introduction of the necessary will and austerity and self-discipline which will give it endurance and purity".[7]

Aurobindo would not consider the synthesis of ethics and culture as the final consummation of man's creative achievements. Both beauty and *ethics* have their genesis in infrarational sources with a vague sense of appreciation of the pleasant and the right. He is not primarily a cultural historian or anthropologist but basically a seeker after *God* and the divine light and power and bliss. His theory of a suprarational good and suprarational beauty beyond culture remains, after all, a transcendental category and not a generalised sociological concept.

Aurobindo has formulated a theory of the decline and fall

of cultures and civilisations. He conceives of a cycle of birth, growth, youth, ripeness and decline for the life of *society*. To him, the European theories of cycles of culture miss the spiritual source of self-prolongation by constant self-renewal which is the principle of immortality. But he finds some scope for its recognition in the growing trend in Europe towards subjectivism. In analysing the causes that lead to the disintegration of civilisations and cultures he emphasises the loss and exhaustion of internal strength and vitality and not the external migrations and invasions of barbarians and foreigners.

Aurobindo's theory of the decline of civilisations and cultures has some remarkable similarities to the Spenglerian morphology of world history. Spengler traces the origin of culture to the spiritual force of the proto-soul. Aurobindo finds even in the primitive stages of humanity the operation of occult and lower vital institutional forces which are only the hidden and subordinate operations of the involved spirit. Both accept that the exhaustion and loss of spiritual forces lead to the decline of culture-cycles. In Spengler one finds a spirit of cosmic pessimism, whereas in Aurobindo there is a profound optimism.

Aurobindo is justified in emphasising the necessity of ethical factors for the growth of a true and harmonious *culture*. Albert Schweitzer strongly stresses the need for an ethical foundation for cultures. The supreme emphasis laid by Aurobindo on the moral governance of life and society reveal his personality as a sage and prophet. He has stressed the transcendence of instinctive vitalism and sensationalistic hedonism by an ethical culture based on discipline, character and cultivation of a strong will for the realisation of the spiritual values. He wants the enshrinement of human and divine values. He has rightly drawn a distinction between civilisation and culture. He deserves full credit to the extent that he is the one foremost Indian thinker who has tried to develop a philosophy of history and culture on the basis of a vast metaphysical structure.

REFERENCES

1. Sri Aurobindo, *The Human Cycle, op. cit.*, p. 2.
2. V.P. Varma, *The Political Philosophy of Sri Aurobindo*, Asia Publishing House, Calcutta, 1960, pp. 138-39.
3. Sri Aurobindo, *The Human Cycle, op. cit.*, p. 15.
4. *Ibid.*, p. 46.
5. Sri Aurobindo, *The Life Divine*, Vol. II, *op. cit.*, p. 658.
6. Sri Aurobindo, *The Human Cycle, op. cit.*, p. 111.
7. *Ibid.*, p. 121.

5

AUROBINDO ON NATIONALISM AND IDEAL OF HUMAN UNITY

Aurobindo was appointed the Principal of the National College at Calcutta in August 1906. His work was two fold; carrying on vigorous propaganda for *nationalism*, and teaching on national lines. He had to suffer imprisonments and persecutions. In 1907 he was prosecuted for sedition but was acquitted. He emphasised the spiritual significance of the nationalist movement in Bengal. Subhas Chandra Bose was greatly influenced by the noble self-sacrifice of Aurobindo and he has definitely stated that Aurobindo was the most popular leader in Bengal during his undergraduate days.

Aurobindo had originally retired from politics in order to obtain increased spiritual strength and vitality for eventual use in the cause of India's independence. In a letter to Romain Rolland, he wrote, "India possesses in its past, a little rusty and out of use, the key to the progress of *humanity*. It is to this side that I am now turning my energies, rather than towards mediocre politics. Hence the reason for my withdrawal. I believe in the necessity for *Tapasya*".[1] After leaving politics, he retained his interest in politics. He wrote two important books on political and social philosophy: The *Human Cycle* and The Ideal of Human Unity. In his pre-Pondicherry days he was primarily a nationalist leader and political prophet, in the Pondicherry days he assumed the role of a political and social thinker and philosopher. He regarded Tilak not as a revolutionist but as a democrat with great mass influence who had definitely Indianised the political movement.

Aurobindo retained a very soft corner for the issues of independence and unification of India. The message that he sent at the death of Mahatma Gandhi contains his prophetic faith in the glory and greatness of India. He said, "The light which led us to freedom, though not yet to unity, still burns and will burn on till it conquers. I believe firmly that a great and united India is the destiny of the nation and its peoples. The power that brought us through so much struggle and suffering to freedom will achieve also, through whatever strife or trouble, the aim which so poignantly occupied the thought of the fallen leader at the time of his tragic ending; as it brought us *freedom*, it will bring us unity. A free and united India will be there and the Mother will gather around her sons and weld them into a single national strength in the life of a great and united people".[2]

Aurobindo's main problem was to preach the cult of spiritual and moral nationalism; violence played an insignificant role in his political prescriptions. Personally he never resorted to armed activities. He did not think in terms of an organised violent *proletarian* or even a lower middle class revolution. He is not comparable to Mazzini in the intensity and range of the latter's political influence. But Mazzini and Aurobindo resemble in their philosophic approach to politics. In his later days Mazzini was intensely critical of *Marxism*. Aurobindo has been critical of western mechanical economism and barbaric materialism. He upholds the theory of the manifestation of the supreme reality in cosmic progression. Both think that *nationalism* is a stage towards cosmopolitanism and human unity and is not something ultimate in itself.

Aurobindo has attempted an analysis and evaluation of the Indian *renaissance* which preceded the growth of Indian nationalism. The eighteenth and early nineteenth centuries in India were periods of political decline, defeat and anarchy marked by the exhaustion and near disintegration of the creative spirit in religion and art. He compares the Indian renaissance not to the European Renaissance of the fifteenth century which signified a seizure of Christianised, Teutorised, feudalised Europe by the Graeco-Roman spirit of unhindered rationalism and independent free enquiry, but to the Celtic Renaissance when Ireland wanted to go back to the other culture after a long period of English domination. In his analysis of the Indian renaissance, he puts the central emphasis on the recovery of the spiritual traditions and heritage of the past.

The establishment of new religious sects in India Aurobindo considers to be a central event in the Indian renaissance. He refers to the *cosmopolitanism, electicism*, religious *rationalism* and logic of the Brahmo Samaj which he considers similar to English unitarianism in some forms. Of all the Indian renaissance leaders the dynamic and spiritual puissancc and fervour of Dayananda appeal to him most and the latter considers him a unique personality trying to create a vigorous Aryan manhood in India. He credits the Theosophical movement for getting some recognition in the West for some of the psychic, occult and esoteric achievements of the old Hindus. He considers Ramakrishna to be the man who had the greatest influence and has done the most to regenerate Bengal.

Aurobindo has been considered the greatest synthesis of the genius of Europe and the genius of Asia. The sage of Pondicherry as Gandhi called him has been considered by Radhakrishnan as the greatest intellectual of our age and a great force in the realm of spirit. He believed that the ever-growing spiritual and intellectual advance of India was bound to come. He said, "The renaissance of India is as inevitable as the rising of tomorrow's sun, and the renaissance of a great nation of three hundred millions with so peculiar a temperament, such unique traditions and ideas of life, so powerful an intelligence and so great a mass of potential energies cannot but be one of the most formidable phenomena of the modern world".[3]

According to Spengler *nationalism* is based upon the tendency to comprehend the infinite both in the spatial and the temporal sense. He says that the eighteenth century marks the emancipation of the national consciousness from the dynastic idea and in this process the French Revolution has a leading significance because it heralded the popular idea in place of the dynastic. Pollard considers the 14th century to be the first epoch of nationalism. Aurobindo finds traces of the first attempts to form a nationality in the Greek city, the Semitic or Mongolian monarchy, the Celtic clan and the Aryan *Kula* or *Jati*. It was the mixture of all these ideas that went to the formation of the medieval nation and evolved the modern peoples.

In the historical process of the formation of the nation-unit Aurobindo emphasises three factors: (i) the role of a strong *kinship*; (2) the role of a fixed social hierarchy; (3) the role of foreign domination. Kingship has played an important role in organising and shaping national life. The nation-unit exists not merely to make political existence possible but is a field for the extension of man's social activities on a larger scale. When these purposes began to be served through different groups and associations and when the people began to assert itself the monarchial external shell was torn and instead of that there began gradually to be enshrined the authority of the vast millions. In the evolution of the nation-unit, the role of kingship has to be recognised. The growth of a solidified hierarchical social structure has also at times been partly responsible for the formation of the nation-unit.

According to Aurobindo, "In medieval India it (the social order) turned towards the social dominance of the sacerdotal class and the substitution of a common spiritual for a common political consciousness as the basis of the national feeling. No lasting secular centre was evolved, no great imperial or kingly head which by its prestige, power, antiguity and claim to general reverence and obedience could over-balance or even merely balance this sacerdotal prestige and predominance and create a sense of political as well as spiritual and cultural oneness".[4] To refute the conception of the connection between social *hierarchy* and the origin of the nation-unit it may very well be said that if social stratification could lead to the formation of the nation-unit it is surprising it should not have done so in the highly stratified societies of Egypt.

According to Aurobindo, foreign domination is the next factor important in the evolution of *nationality* and the nation-state. The histories of Russia and England show the domination of an alien conquering group which transformed itself into a ruling class and was ultimately absorbed in the general population. In many European countries one can find the influence of foreign conquest and rule as a factor leading to the growth of nationality.

Aurobindo distinguishes the pre-national empire-building cycle of the ancient world from the modern cycle of nation-building. There are two types of empires in history. In the homogeneous national empire there is not present any sense of separatism and localism in the component units. On the other hand, in the heterogeneous composite empire the sense of ethnic and cultural particularism continues to operate. There are three important differences between the modern cycle of nation-building and the ancient cycle of empire-building. First, the ancient world developed from the local and regional unit to the imperial conglomeration without evolving the nation-unit. The modern European cycle of nation-building does not overshoot itself by proceeding towards a larger unification to the neglect of the necessary intermediate aggregate. Secondly, the European nation-building cycle represents a growing political evolution through several successive steps. Feudalism provided to Europe a period of the balancing of centripetal and centrifugal forces. The third distinct feature in the modern European nation-building cycle is that it is marked by a process of revolt, resistance and rebellion against too much of authoritarianism.

Aurobindo has drawn a theoretical distinction between peoples and nations. The Asiatic civilisations even during their most organised and flourishing political periods have been characterised by a predominant social, religious and cultural ethos and not by the politicism implied in the modern nation-states. They have been national "only in the sense of having a common soul-life, a common culture, a common social organisation, a common political head, but not nation-states".[5] In Tagore we find a distinction between nations and peoples.

Aurobindo sometimes says that nationalism in India is eternal because *Sanatana Dharma* is eternal, and *Sanatana Dharma* is nationalism. He refers to the Rajputs, especially of Mewar, 'to whom the Rajah was in every way the head of the society and of the nation'. *Political nationalism* in the sense that a people linked by a feeling of common belongingness should have the power of autonomous political self-determination, is definitely a western phenomenon. Cultural nationalism, in the sense of a broad fundamental unity running throughout the history and culture of the peoples may be traced in the historical evolution of India. But India has taken the concept of national self-determination from the west.

According to Aurobindo, one can trace a centripetal tendency throughout Indian history. He said, "The political history of India is the story of a succession of empires, indigenous and foreign, each of them destroyed by centrifugal forces, but each bringing the centripetal tendency nearer to its triumphant emergence. And it is a significant circumstance that the more foreign the rule, the greater has been its force for the unification of the subject people. This is always a sure sign that the essential nation-unit is already there and that there is an indissoluble national vitality necessitating the inevitable emergence of the organised nation".[6]

Aurobindo refers to the vital basis of the *clan* and the *tribe*. The foundations and the essential elements of nationality are a geographical unity, a common past and a powerful common interest to him. But a common enthusiasm coalescing with a common interest is the most powerful fosterer of nationality. To him, unity of race, religion or language is not indispensable to nationality. He said, "It is true that nationhood still founds itself largely on the idea of race, but this is in the nature of a fiction. It covers the historical fact of a fusion of many races and attributes a natural motive to a historical and geographical association".[7] In his writings one finds the word race constantly used but it always signifies the sense of people or humanity at large. He never accepts the biological concept of different races with their different natural propensities and *soul*. Several nation-states may pride themselves on their racial homogeneity as constituting the basis of their unity, but among the elements constituting nationality he stresses not the vital principle of race but the concept of psychological unity.

Aurobindo lays the emphasis on the psychological rather than on the biological and physical principle as the foundation of *nationality*. To him, nationhood refers primarily to the idea of psychological unity, which, in turn, might be accentuated by common historical memories of ancient traditions, past heroes and sufferings, by common geographical habitation and by common interests and values. He said, "The nation is a persistent psychological unit which Nature has been busy developing throughout the world in the most various forms and educating into physical and political unity. . . . All modern attempts to destroy by force or break up a nation are foolish and futile, because they ignore the law of natural evolution. Empires are still perishable political units; the nation is immortal".[8]

Although Aurobindo is emphatic in considering the psychological element as the dominant factor in the *constitution* of the nation, he does not support the growth of national egoism. There can be various factors on which the sentiment of collective national egoism can base itself. He condemns modern capitalism and imperialism because in place of serving the legitimate interests of the people and the country they aggrandise the pride, insolence and chauvinism of nations and preach the dangerous slogans of race superiority. Due to the virulent operation of imperialistic jingoism, injustice, *exploitation* and oppression are resorted to "and by that fatal progression which the Greeks so clearly demarcated, it leads from prosperity to insolence and outrage and from insolence and outrage to eat, that blind infatuation which is God's instrument for the destruction of men and nations".[9] In the accentuation of national egoism he finds the seeds of moral and political fall and catastrophe.

Aurobindo's psychological concept of nationhood always involves a reference to the spiritual factor. He does not accept a behaviourist and materialist or functional approach to the social sciences. He wants the subconscious power of the group-soul, which has been operating so long as a subterranean element, to be brought to the surface and made an active force. He refers to the new influence of subjectivism on the *nationalism* which had developed in the previous rationalistic era. He said, "The nascent subjectivism preparative of the new age has shown itself in the new collective self-consciousness of man in that organic mass of his life which he has most firmly developed in the past, the nation".[10]

Aurobindo develops the theory of the soul of the nation at great length. A nation which has once risen, once has been called up by the voice of God to rise cannot be checked, in the course of the discovery of its soul through processes of cultural creativeness and political independence, by physical repression. He states that even in those who were opposing the movement and obstructing its successful consummation God himself was working. He says that the *nation* is the self-manifestation of the cosmic spirit. He said, "This (society or community or nation) too is a being, a living power of the eternal truth, a self-manifestation of the cosmic spirit, and it is there to express and fulfil in its own way and to the degree of its capacities the special truth and powers and meaning of the cosmic spirit that is within it".[11]

Spiritualism imparted to the Bengal movement a deep political consciousness. Aurobindo referred to the realisation of God in the nation. He said, "Your common Mother. That is not merely the soil. That is not merely a division of land but it is a living thing. It is the Mother in whom you move and have your being. Realise God in the nation, realise God in your brother, realise God in a wide human association".[12] Again, he said, "The three hundred millions of people of this country are God in the nation, something which cannot be measured by so much land, or by so much money, or by so many lives. You will then realise that it is something immortal, that the idea for which you are working is something immortal and that it is an immortal power that is working in you".[13] This realisation of the immortal power and spirit of the Divine Being as manifesting itself on the political plane through a rising nation was to be achieved by a total surrender and consecration of oneself to the great cause.

According to Aurobindo the Indian nation was to achieve unity not by the European method of emphasis on common self-interest but by feeling of love, veneration and devotion for and to the country. Above all, the people were to be united by the feeling that we are all sons of one common Mother who is also the manifestation of God in a United *Humanity*. He accepted the idea of the spiritual motherland under divine supervision even in his early days. The great prominence of the concept of the divine motherland in his political speeches and in his own personal convictions reveals and reflects the strong influence of the religious traditions of India.

The theory of the nation-soul and the concept of the nation as the self-revolution of the cosmic spirit, as found in Aurobindo, is partly similar to the concept of *nationalism* developed by Fichte and Hegel. According to Aurobindo, the nation is regarded as the manifestation of the divine mother while the state is only a mechanical contrivance assuming supremacy in a rational age. Both Aurobindo and Hegel are similar to the extent that they accept the manifestation of the Welt-Geist in the historical process of the evolution of the nation. They both accept that the spirit or the Geist provides the central dynamic force to the other diverse activities of the nation.

Aurobindo accepts the theory of the divinity of the nation. He conceives of the *nation* as the manifestation of the divine mother. He accepts the spiritual concept of the realisation of God in the nation, and also beyond the nation, in humanity. In his political philosophy, he did never become as outspoken and fanatical as that. He does not make an absolute apothesis of the nation-state. Since he accepts the idea of the divine motherhood of the nation, he is not worried by the problem of the divergence of the mutual interests of the individual and the nation. To him, the individual also is divine, if the nation is divine; and hence both being aspects of the same being, the nation is only a stage for the divine fulfilment of the individual.

Aurobindo upheld that God was manifesting Himself through India, the common mother. This belief implied that all types of local and partial loyalties to the ego, the family and the class, were to be forsaken for the cause of the larger national self. According to Aurobindo, nationalism is a religion that has come from God, and therefore this creed has to be lived and practised in a spirit of humility and dedication and not of intellectual arrogance. *Nationalism* has not been crushed. Nationalism is not going to be crushed. Nationalism survives in the strength of God and hence it could not be defeated, no matter howsoever invincible the forces against it might appear to be. Bengal nationalism was not the mere imitation of the European prototype. Nationalism was not the mere pursuit of collective political self-interest. It was a religion of the realisation of the cosmic being through the nation. Thus in its innermost nature the nationalist movement was not inspired by any self-interest.

The intellect is an important device for social action. It can neither inspire followers nor can it create the heroic leader. The intellect does not conquer nature and destiny, lay its hand on the future, command the world. This emphasis laid by Aurobindo on the failure of the intellect to provide the necessary impetus and inspiration in the realm of actual political dynamics and historical creativism shows that for the rise and liberation of nations what is needed is not the scientific analysis of logical and causal interconnections but the mystic and mighty faith in the destiny of the nation. He supports his thesis of the necessity of an intuitional faith in the destiny of the nation and the divine leadership of the country by stressing the inadequacy of mere industrial and material progress. The latter represents only the external shell.

Aurobindo emphasised the necessity of *Sadhana* and *Jnana*. *Sadhana* signifies the process of spiritual identification with the source and primal centre of spiritual energy. It would enable the political leaders and followers to establish contact with the divine being who was the ultimate leader and captain of the movement. *Jnana* means not an acquisition of intellectual knowledge but the realisation of a spiritual vision and inward perception which can enable a person to look into the depths and find out the mainsprings of action in nature and society. *Jnana* transcends the mere logical analysis of objects and phenomena by the discursive intellect.

Aurobindo stressed the cultivation of moral virtues and spiritual techniques, not only for the purpose of obtaining inward strength and purification but also as conservers of national vitality and power. He declared that nationalism is a *Dharma* and at times struggle, battle and even murder could be part of *Dharma*, but not hatred and jealousy. From the standpoint of individual moral growth and social development he stated that jealousy and hatred should be given up. Nevertheless, he was also a realist and thought that if occasionally, in a big political movement, sentiments of hatred were generated and expressed, the whole movement could not be condemned. The Aurobindian conception of *nationalism* as a religion has a strong resemblance to the Mazzinian conception. There is nothing definite to show the influence of

Mazzini on Aurobindo's theory of nationalism as a religion.

Aurobindo modified his older conception of nationalism as a *religion*. He began to emphasise that *Sanatana Dharma* itself was nationalism. He said that the cosmic spirit was moving towards the realisation of an all-embracing world-religion which would have its basis in the wider *Hinduism*. The *Sanatana Dharma* signified the eternal truths and principles of human life and the cosmos, and of this body of knowledge India has always been destined to be the guardian, exemplar and missionary. He said, "I say no longer that nationalism is a creed, a religion, a faith; I say that it is the *Sanatana Dharma* which for us is nationalism. This Hindu nation was born with the *Sanatana Dharma*, with it, it moves and with it, it grows. When the *Sanatana Dharma* declines then the nation declines and if the *Sanatana Dharma* were capable of perishing, with the *Sanatana Dharma* it would perish. The *Sanatana Dharma*, that is nationalism".[14]

This new conception of *Sanatana Dharma* as nationalism modified the political character of the earlier conception of *nationalism* as a pure and *Sattvic* religion. This change in political theory was a reflection of the change in Aurobindo's personality. Before he went to prison, he revealed a greater political keenness and realism. After his return, politics became subservient to spiritualism. The new conception of *Sanatana Dharma* as nationalism had two sociological aspects. First, it was a powerful message of religious revival. Secondly, it was strongly suffused with elements of messianism. He wanted the revival of the spirit, ideals and methods of the ancient India in a yet more effective form and with a more modern organisation.

Aurobindo was not a blind worshipper of the past. He discerns three elements in all life. First, a fixed and permanent spirit which cannot be changed but may sometimes be lost or obscured. Secondly, a developing yet constant soul which should not be rashly meddled with Thirdly, the brittle mutable body which was to be used as an instrument. He was against any imitation. He wanted India to be faithful to her real self, and she could be true to herself only if she discovered her genuine soul which was manifested in the ancient scriptures. He insisted on the recovery of the *Veda, Vedanta*, the *Yoga* and the *Tantra*. He did not stand for an utter condemnation of the European civilisation. He was only opposed to the dominating secularistic and imperialistic stamp of the *Occident*. He wanted to pursue the study of European civilisation from the Indian standpoint. He wanted that the supreme gospels of ancient India should become the central ideational theme in the new political movement.[15]

According to Aurobindo, "Indians, it is the spirituality of India, the *Sadhana* of India, *Tapasya, Jnanam, Sakti* that must make us free and great. And these great things of the East are ill rendered by their inferior English equivalents, discipline, philosophy, strength. *Tapasya* is more than discipline, it is the materialisation in ourselves, by spiritual means, of the divine energy, creative, preservative and destructive. *Jnanam* is more than philosophy, it is the inspired and direct knowledge which comes of what our ancients called *dristi*, spiritual sight. *Sakti* is more than strength, it is the universal energy which moves the stars, made individual. It is the East that must conquer in India's uprising. It is the *Yogin* who must stand behind the political leader or manifest within him; Ramdas must be born in one body with Shivaji, Mazzini mingle with Cavour".[16]

Aurobindo wanted the people of India to attain national maturity, moral strength and confidence. He did not stand for any social conservatism and reaction. He was opposed not to change but to the irrational imitation of the West. Indian society might have to undergo a thorough reconstruction, amounting even to a revolution, but it would not be a Europeanisation.

The belief in the sanctity of spiritual values has been very strong in Ramakrishna, Dayananda, Aurobindo and Gandhi. Aurobindo is emphatic in his assertion that political success cannot be achieved without the incorporation of spiritual and moral values in life. The spiritual concepts of *Tapasya, Jnana* and *Sakti* are essential not only for the salvation of the soul but are also vital elements for the achievement of success in political struggles. He is a perfect believer in the spiritualist theory of politics. He is fully convinced that unless fundamental spiritual norms are incorporated into the political and social life of the country, India cannot rise to great heights. He wants India to be not just a mere pale replica of Europe.

The revivalistic emphasis on the nation's being true to its real self is very strong in Aurobindo's political philosophy. In modern times the revivalistic element has been strong in Ramakrishna, Dayananda, Vivekananda, Ramtirtha, Tilak, Aurobindo and Gandhi. Revivalism can operate both in the social and religious fields. Assessing the role and orientation of Tilak as a political leader, Aurobindo said, "The peculiar role which he has played as a trusted and accredited leader of conservative and religious India in the path of democratic politics. It was his position which enabled him to effect the union of the new political spirit with the tradition and sentiment of the historic past and of both with the ineradicable religious temperament of the people of which these festivals were the symbol".[17] He stood for the revival of the spirit of the *Vedanta*, the *Yoga* and the *Tantra*.

There were several sociological and historical factors responsible for the dominant religious and revivalistic orientation of Indian nationalism. First, the continuing power of Brahmanical ecclesiasticism, as the repository of the sacred wisdom of old, over the mind of India was a great factor. The decline of Buddhism which contained more rational and critical elements in it had left the field clear for the sway of the old religious and philosophic thought. Secondly, while in Europe the rise of nationalism on a large scale was marked by the preceding growth of a powerful rationalistic philosophy, the nationalistic movement in India arose in the wake of a religious and ethical *revivalism*. Thirdly, the presence of a militant, powerful Moslem minority in India always made the religious question very acute. The British imperialistic policy of divide and rule intensified the separatist consciousness which by antipathetic reaction accentuated revivalism. The Moslem minority was very sensitive for fear of being suppressed, due to the probable chances of political victory of the Hindu majority. Although the Hindu Moslem controversy did not play an important role in the Bengal nationalist movement of 1905-10, he considered the differences between the two communities to be a factor hindering the growth of nationalism in India.

According to Aurobindo, *Sanatana Dharma* did not signify any narrow creed. Although the *Vedas*, the *Vedanta*, the *Gita*, the *Yoga*, the *Tantra* and the *Puranas* were the basic scriptures of Hinduism, the *Sanatana Dharma* which is the basis of the future world-religion, towards which the world-spirit was moving, could not reject even the *Bible* or the *Koran*. The real scripture, however, that was fully authentic was the human heart wherein the divine himself dwelt.[18] He stressed that in order to be the basis and spiritual foundation of the future world-religion, Hinduism had to be dynamic. He said, "Hinduism has always been pliable and aggressive, it has thrown itself on the attacking force, carried its positions, plundered its treasures, made its own everything of value it had and ended in wholly annexing it or driving it out by rendering its future continuance in the country purposeless and therefore impossible".[19]

Aurobindo envisaged the possibility of a new synthesis of the *Vedanta*, Samkara's being only one synthesis revealing the austere monism of its gospel but by no means exhausting all the possible synthesis that could be evolved out of the *Vedanta*. He even began to assert that the real aim of the nationalist movement was not the mere achievement of political autonomy and independence but the expansion of Indian civilisation. He referred to the crossing of the geographical limits of Asia by the gospel of the *Vedanta* and the *Yoga*, which had even gone to Europe and America. He did not visualise a political or military conquest but a spiritual conquest, something like the one attempted by Buddhism.

According to Aurobindo, *Yoga* meant not external austerities and physical askesis but an inward transfiguration and divinisation of man's central being. The real problem by inwards and not in external nature and society. The true solution lay not in progressive control over the external world through manipulating the resources of science and technology, but in making a conquest of one's self. He believed that Asia and India were rising not for the sake of comfort and luxury but for vindicating the freedom of man within as well as without. It was for completing this profound moral and spiritual work that India claimed her destined freedom and greatness and it was to the interest of all humanity not excluding England, that she should wholly establish her claim. He said, "We believe. . . . that India is destined to work out her own independent life and civilisation, to stand in the forefront of the world and solve the political, social, economic and moral problems which Europe has failed to solve, yet the pursuit of which and the feverish passage in that pursuit from experiment to experiment, from failure to failure, she calls her progress".[20]

Aurobindo felt that the world was getting ready for a new spiritual dispensation and India was to be the heralder of a new gospel and Weltanschauung. He was opposed to the mere imitation of the techniques and ideas of the western nations. He refused to be satisfied with the emphasis being placed only on political independence. He always held a dynamic conception of the *spirit* which manifests itself through nature and life and mind. He re-emphasised the spiritual role of India in the world. He said, "India was not to be a nation like many others evolving an opulent industry and commerce, a powerful organisation of social and political life, an immense military strength, practising power politics with a high degree of success, guarding and extending jealously her gains and her interests, dominating over a large part of the world, but in this apparently magnificent progression forfeiting its *Svadharma*, losing its *soul*. Then ancient India and her spirit might disappear altogether and we have only one more nation like the others and that would be a real gain neither to the world nor to us. . . . It would be a tragic irony of fate, if India were to throw away her spiritual heritage at the very moment when in the rest of the world there is more and more a turning towards her for spiritual help and a saving light".[21]

In 1950 Aurobindo remarked, "India is free and her freedom was necessary if the Divine work was to be done. The difficulties that surround her and may increase for a time, especially with regard to the Pakistan imbroglio, were also things that had to come and to be cleared out. . . . Afterwards, the work for the *Divine* will become more possible and it may well be that the dream, if it is a dream, of leading the world towards the spiritual light, may even become a reality".[22] Ram Mohan wanted India even to adopt English as the universal language and then to achieve independence and enlighten the rest of Asia. Ramatirtha stressed the greatness of the monistic philosophy of the *Vedanta* and its imperative necessity for the peoples of the world. Tagore spoke of the universalism of the spiritual message of India to the West. Gandhi thought that India was rising to prove to the world the superior moral efficacy of non-violence. According to Spengler monotheism, messianism and the concept of the chosen people are basic Magian ideas.

The rise of *nationalism* and the growth of a new social and political faith and fervour got mixed up with the older conception of the messiah. In the political messianism of the 19th century the idea of a whole nation as messiah developed instead of the older idea of a personal messiah or redeemer. Commenting upon the messianic elements in 19th century nationalism, Hans Kohn said, "The nation transcends the limits of a social or political concept; it becomes a holy body sanctified by God, and nationalism is no longer a political loyalty which can be changed according to social circumstances and convictions but becomes a religious duty full of responsibility towards God and the redemption.".[23]

Nationalistic or religious *messianism* is born out of and rationalises social and political frustrations and deprivations. It is a product both of frustration and of faith. When the chances of success are completely absent there is utter hopelessness and despair, and a spirit of calm resignation and silent surrender prevails. But when there are even remote chances of future success, the tendency arises to interpret present suffering as only a means for some future purpose. Indian nationalistic messianism has been a rationalisation of the periods of persecution, suffering and wounded pride. Hindu culture had been exposed to tremendous onslaughts from foreigners. All other foreign elements had been assimilated and absorbed by Hinduism except the Moslems. The Indian people were facing a dangerous threat to their sense of self-esteem and their residues of personal, social and national integrity. Messianism developed as a necessary counterpoise to political and economic subjection. Aurobindo, although he accepts the synthesis of the ascetic emphasis on the quest of the spirit and the materialistic emphasis on life, has always stressed the moral and spiritual greatness of India and has propounded the view that the ultimate regeneration of the world would come only through the spiritual light shed by Indian sages.

Buddha and Dayananda preached the supremacy and the efficacy of their religious teachings. There was no idea in them of a group or a country being specially commissioned by some higher power to spread that gospel in the world. Aurobindo said, "One of the oldest races and greatest civilisation on this earth, the most indomitable in vitality, the most fecund in greatness, the deepest in life, the most wonderful in potentiality. . . . is sure to succeed because the freedom, unity and greatness of India have now become necessary to the world".[24] This nationalistic messianism of Aurobindo seems to run counter to his transcendentalistic and universalistic *Vendantism*. He attributes a dynamic nature to the absolute, accepts the concept of the Welt-Geist in history and also preaches the creed of the spirit of the nation. It is true that he is not a narrow nationalist and goes beyond Hegel in accepting the idea of humanity and cosmopolitanism, and even formulates his plans of human unity.

Aurobindo was a preacher of Political Vedantism and *passive resistance*. He said, "I have adopted the principles of the political philosophy of the West and I have assimilated that to the immortal teachings of *Vedantism*".[25] He has tried to interpret some of the spiritual concepts of Vedantic philosophy in a political context. Vivekananda and Ramatirtha formulated the conception of practical Vedanta as the way to success in individual and national life. Aurobindo expounds the philosophy of Political Vedantism. Vivekananda and Aurobindo have defended the *Vedanta* from the charge of being neutral to ethics and have regarded the *Vedanta* to be basis of the highest morality. Vedantic spiritualism has been invoked in modern India to preach racial equality and the abolition of untouchability.

Vivekananda preached the greatness of the Vedanta as the only system of religion and philosophy which could not only stand the onslaughts of science but could give a larger meaning even to science. He felt that the electro-magnetic theory was advancing science in the direction of *Vedanta*. The political and social implication that he drew from the Vedanta was remarkable in its insistence on strength as the remedy for all evils and misery in the world. Aurobindo interprets the Vedanta as containing an exalted conception of life. He said, "The dignity of human existence, given to it by the thought of the Vedantic and the classical ages of Indian *culture*, exceeded anything conceived by the noblest idea of humanity. Man is a spirit veiled in the works of energy and moving to self-discovery".[26] The aim of man according to the Vedanta is to become perfection and to attain unity with the cosmic and transcendental being.

According to Aurobindo, the Vedanta is not merely a philosophy of the cosmos and of the transcendent being and awareness but it also contains the seeds of national emancipation because it provides a metaphysical defence of the idea of the country as the Mother and as divine. The motherland is only a power of the ultimate reality; it is the goddess, the mother of the world, *Kali*. He refers to the great Vedantic concept of *Maya*. The *Maya* of the alien civilisation was triumphant in India and *Mukti* signified political freedom. He said, "We in India fell under the influence of the foreigners' *Maya* which completely possessed our souls. It was the *Maya* of the alien rule, the alien civilisation, the powers and capacities of the alien people who happen to rule over us".[27]

Aurobindo equates Political Vedantism with ethical relativism and neutrality, bordering almost upon *Machiavellism*. He said, Vedantism accepts no distinction of true or false religions, but considers only what will lead more or less quickly to *Moksha*, spiritual emancipation and the realisation of the Divinity within. Our attitude is political *Vedantism*. India, free, one and indivisible, is the divine realisation to which we move, —emancipation is our aim; to that end each nation must practise the political creed which is best suited to its temperament and circumstances; for that is best for it which leads most surely and compietely to national liberty and national self-realisation".[28] The basic argument of Aurobindo is that metaphysical Vedantism teaches the concept of the spiritual realisation of the absolute, and that being the central aim and the only goal it accepts no distinction between true or false religions but only considers what would be the quickest and the most certain technic of *Moksha*. The implication is drawn therefrom that Political Vedantism should concentrate on the main objective of political emancipation and each nation should choose the means best suited to its temperament and the objective situation and environment.

Aurobindo emphasises the fundamental importance of the basic aim of progress towards national emancipation and upholds that no method or action is politically good or evil except as it helps or hinders the goal. The Political Vedantism of Aurobindo has Machiavellian implications. Aurobindo is evolving Political Vedantism to support the thesis that at times armed revolt could become necessary against the constituted authority. His Political Vedantism is aimed against the supporters of unadulterated pacifism and non-violence, and since the latter quote the maxim non-violence is the ultimate religion, Aurobindo resorts to his Political Vedantism.

Aurobindo supported active resistance. He said, "The *Gita* is the best answer to those who shrink from battle as a sin and aggression as a lowering of morality".[29] He also referrred at times to the *Svadharma* of the *Kshatriya*. The morality of the warrior caste teaches violence in times of war; boycott being a kind of war, violence was justified therein. He said that the Indian leaders were averse to following the American precedent, not on moral grounds, but because the political situation was not favourable. He said, "Justice and righteousness are the atmosphere of political morality but the justice and righteousness of the fighter, not of the priest. Aggression is unjust only when unprovoked".[30] Again, "*Liberty* is the fruit we seek from the sacrifice, and the Motherland the goddess to whom we offer it; into the seven leaping tongues of the fire of the *yajna* we must after all that we are and all that we have feeding the fire even with our blood and lives and happiness of our nearest and dearest; for the Motherland is a goddess who loves not a maimed and imperfect sacrifice, and freedom was never won from the gods by a grudging giver".[31]

On the basis of the ancient teachings of the *Gita*, Aurobindo advocated violence in retaliation. He said, "If the instruments of the executive choose to disperse our meetings by breaking the heads of those present, the right of self-defence entitles us not merely to defend our heads but to retaliate on those of the head-breakers. . . . Nor does resistance pass into the aggressive stage so long as it resists coercive violence in its own kind and confines itself to repelling attack. . . . Nor is it inclined to be hysterical over a few dozen of broken heads".[32] He referred constantly to the classical arguments of Krishna who passionately condemned Arjuna's wish to desist from battle because it would entail violence to kinsmen. He supported the use of violence by the Russian revolutionaries and the Irish *patriots*.

According to Aurobindo, "Passive resistance cannot build up a strong and great nation unless it is masculine, bold and ardent in its spirit and ready at any moment and at the slightest notice to supplement itself with active resistance. We do not want to develop a nation of women who know only how to suffer and not how to strike".[33] He supported political violence and armed revolt not only on grounds of the social vocation or *Dharma* of Kshatriya, but also with reference to the philosophic theory of the cosmic destruction by *Mahakali* as developed in the *Puranas* and *Tantra*. His support of active resistance and boycott brings out the realistic character of his political philosophy. He defended boycott as a legitimate political technique against the attacks of Tagore. His concept of politics as the *Dharma* of the Kshatriya also demonstrates his realism.

Aurobindo extends the *Gita* concept of *Svadharma*. The *Gita* refers only to the *Dharma* of individuals, determined with reference to the *Varna* they belong to. According to Aurobindo, groups, and even the nation, have their *Svadharma*. He also spoke at times of the *Yugadharma*. He denied that philanthropy and humanitarianism were a part of his *Yoga*. The main object of *Yoga* was not social service but the attainment of divine consciousness. He said, "I do not know why you drag in humanitarianism, activism, philanthropy, *seva*, etc. None of these are part of my *Yoga* or in harmony with my works, so that they do not touch me. I never thought that politics or feeding the poor. . . . would lead straight to the Absolute".[34] He accepted that "all that seeks, all that finds, all that voices or figures is a realisation of something of the play of the Infinte and to that extent can be made a means of God-realisation or of divine formation".[35] During his early nationalist days he considered *Yoga* to be the supreme means of political success. To him, the *Gita* does not teach social service but the doctrine of transfiguration of man into a willing agent of the divine, and hence it preaches spiritualised divine action.

Aurobindo made an intense and passionate appeal for *passive resistance*. He was against the Moderates' theory of politics of petition. In place of prayer, petition, protest and please, he advocated the more radical policy of boycott. He was realistic enough to visualise that if other nations had won the precious prize of liberty by intense suffering, humiliations and martyrdom, then merely by spending the ink of the journalist and petition-framer and the breadth of the orator India could not advance one yard nearer to freedom. He condemned the politics of petitioning as the dream of timid inexperience, the teaching of false friends who hope to keep us in perpetual subjection, foolish to reason, false to experience. To him, the moderates displayed only a spirit of sentimental moral enthusiasm or at least an inoffensive philanthropic patriotism. He condemned the imitative trends of Indian politics in the nineteenth century and the domination of English books.

Aurobindo outlined three important conditions for national progress through the actualisation of *Swaraj*. First, an unhindered intellectual growth and independent motion and action which only could encourage and foster national progress by providing an antithesis to the fatal dependence, passivity and helplessness into which the country had fallen. Secondly, the organisation of the national will in a strong central authority. Thirdly, organised resistance. A nation could vindicate its desire for autonomous political existence in three ways. First, there was the traditional method of armed military revolt or insurrection. Secondly, organised aggressive resistance. Thirdly, passive resistance. He draws a distinction between passive and aggressive resistance.

Aggressive resistance entails the resistance to an unjust law by the destruction of the mechanism which makes and supports that law. *Passive resistance*, on the other hand, aims at rendering ineffective the institution and operation of an unjust law. It concentrates upon organised disobedience to a harsh law and thereby insists upon its withdrawal. Aurobindo said, "A law imposed by a people on itself has a binding force which cannot be ignored except under extreme necessity; a law imposed from outside has no such moral sanction; its claim to obedience must rest on coercive force or on its own equitable and beneficial character and not on the source from which it proceeds. If it is unjust and oppressive, it may become a duty to disobey it and quietly endure the punishment which the law has provided for its violation".[36]

There were three canons of *passive resistance*. First, to break an unjust coercive law is not only justifiable but under given circumstances it could become a duty. Secondly, to resist an unjust executive order or coercive interference could be not only justifiable but under certain circumstances became a duty. Thirdly, the social boycott and excommunication of traitors and others who engaged in treasonable activities against the nation were legitimate. Aurobindo referred to the moral side of passive resistance. He said, "Passive resistance may be the final method of salvation in our case or it may be only the preparation for the final *Sadhana*. In either case, the sooner we put it into full and perfect practice, the nearer shall we be to national liberty".[37]

Aurobindo who was a believer in Political Vedantism and *Dharma-Yuddha* frankly stated that if passive resistance failed active resistance should be resorted to. He would not stress passivity at the cost of resistance. He sanctioned retaliation on the head-breakers. If the police authorities or unofficial hooligans themselves become rioters and breakers of the peace, passive resistance is suspended and active resistance becomes a duty.

Aurobindo not only preached passive resistance, he advocated complete independence for India. He advocated a free constitutional and democratic system of Government for India and pleaded for the entire removal of foreign control and for the achievement of perfect national liberty. He said, "Our ideal is that of *Swarajya* or absolute autonomy free from foreign control. We claim the right of every nation to live its own life by its own energies according to its own nature and ideals. We reject the claim of aliens to force upon us a civilisation inferior to our own or to keep us out of our inheritance on the untenable ground of a superior fitness".[38] He was against the acceptance of colonial self-government as the final objective of India's political efforts.

Aurobindo was inspired by the concept of *self-determination* as loudly proclaimed during the First World War. It was hoped that a purely psychological principle of free will and free choice would be the bond of social and political cohesiveness instead of the vital basis of political and economic needs and pressures. He said, "The Russian principle belongs, in fact to a possible future in which moral and psychological principles will have a real chance to dominate, and vital and physical necessities will have to suit themselves to them instead of, as now, the other way round; it belongs to an arrangement of things that would be the exact reverse of the present international system".[39] Nevertheless he felt that the Russian principle of a confederation of free self-determining nationalities contained seeds of development for the near future.

Aurobindo has condemned European *egoism* and *chauvinism* for intensifying the imperialistic drives of the aggressive powers. Imperialism is an old phenomenon in human history. Spengler held that imperialism is the inevitable stage of human history when culture becomes transformed into a megalopolitan materialistic civilisation. According to Lenin, imperialism is a stage of *capitalism*. According to Kautsky, imperialism is a policy of capitalism. Imperialism cannot be regarded as a solely modern phenomenon. A theory of imperialism which does not take into consideration the political aggressions and conquering designs of peoples and empires in ancient and medieval periods cannot be an adequate explanation of the phenomenon. Aurobindo approaches the problem of imperialism from a psychological-political standpoint. According to him, empires are only political and not real units. He thinks that imperialism represents the aggressive expansion of the national ego.

Aurobindo believed that the imperialistic *egoism* of the great powers would have to cope increasingly with the rising concept of self-determination. The latter alone could be the foundation of a free world-union. Meanwhile he had hoped that the "old, artificial, merely political empire may be replaced by a truer and more moral type, and that the existing empires, driven by the necessity of strengthening themselves and by an enlightened self-interest, may come to see that the recognition of national autonomy is a wise and necessary concession to the still vital instinct of nationalism".[40]

Aurobindo advocates *cosmopolitanism* and world-union. There should be two stages in the life of a nation. In the first stage which is the process of national unification and solidification, the dominant interests of the national unit can preponderate over other local and sectional loyalties and obligations. In the second stage when the nation has become organised and powerful it should minimise its parochial and territorial claims and should preserve itself in a cosmopolitan organisation without destroying the existence as a unit, just as the individual preserves himself in the family, the family in the class and the class in the nation.

Aurobindo always advocated a national religion which we also believe to be universal. He never considers patriotism to be narrow fanatical jingoism or chauvinism but envisages the ultimate unity of mankind. But this unity can be established only on the basis of equality and not of domination by some powers over the others. He always insisted upon the purification of the national movement by concentrating upon the positive national achievements. He believes that human unity is inevitable and he supports it on metaphysical grounds. He said, "Unity is an idea which is not at all arbitrary or unreal, for unity is the very basis of existence. The oneness that is secretly at the foundation of all things, the evolving spirit in Nature, is moved to realise consciously at the top; the evolution moves through diversity, from a simple to a complex oneness. Unity the race moves towards and must one day achieve".[41]

Aurobindo advocates a harmonious synthesis of unity and freedom. He makes a distinction between particularism and separatism. The spirit of particularism can co-exist with unity and can lead to the growth of a healthy spirit of national self-consciousness, but separatist feelings and tendencies are dangerous for a true world union. He would point out three stages in the growth of internationalism. He would not stand for a rigidly mechanical and centralised world state because this would mean only the external form and not the spirit of unity. He is critical of a world state and favours a world union.

Aurobindo advocates a world union based upon the principle of multiple variation and *liberty* and enshrining the concept of a free and rational unity. He specifies four conditions for a free world union. First, the stopping of war as the instrument and mechanism of solving political problems. Secondly, the recognition and concretisation of the right of self-determination for all peoples. Thirdly, the ordering of the economic life of people by mutual and common agreement and not by authoritarian dictation and imposition. Fourthly, the adherence to and propagation of a religion of humanity which is the basic psychological foundation of a world union. He accepts the great contributions of the western mind in evolving the idea of humanity. He said, "The idea of humanity as a single race of being with a common life and a common general interest is among the most characteristic and significant products of modern thought. It is an outcome of the European mind".[42] The religion of *humanity* was born in the rationalistic and philosophical enlightenment movement of the eighteenth century.

Aurobindo pleads for the spiritualisation of the concept of humanity. What he is advocating is not a universal intellectualised religious creed to be accepted by all peoples, but a growing realisation of the omnipresence of a secret, spiritual, all-governing power and reality and the deep consciousness that humanity is its highest present vehicle on earth and that human beings are the means by which it will progressively reveal itself here. He holds that man is the highest creation of the evolutionary progression, but he believes in the inevitable emergence of a gnostic race of superman who will operate through powers far higher and far more subliminal than the limited mind of man. He accepts a synthesis of *Yoga* which integralises gnosis, devotion, psychological introspection and action. He lays the emphasis on a total inward surrender to the divine mother.

Aurobindo does not advocate humanism in the French and German sense of an anti-theological reaction against the dogmatics of Christian theology and the stress on the conception of man as the supreme centre of attention. Man is not ultimate in his scheme. Whatever importance he has is due only to the fact that he expresses the divine. Whatever humanism we find in his thought refers to the derivation of man's importance from the divine spirit. In his earlier writings he proclaimed that the *Sanatana Dharma* could be the foundation of a world religion which alone could save humanity. In his later writings on *Yoga* and philosophy he has laid the central emphasis on a spiritual transmutation of man and a progressive integral reorganisation of the social structure by the incorporation of spiritual powers.

There are several, contributions from Aurobindo as a

theorist of nationalism and as a nationalist leader. He considered the nation as a spiritual subtotality but always treated the state as a machine. His writings reveal that *nationalism* is not a purely political or an economic phenomenon. In his emphasis on *Swadeshi*, he accepts the validity of the economic grounds of nationalism. He conceived of nationalism as a pure *Sattvic* religion and hence he stressed the necessity of spiritual and moral discipline both for the leaders and the followers. He always conceived of nationalism as a stage in the social and political evolution of man. He also simultaneously accepts the realisation of the gospel of human unity as an imperative political necessity for mankind.

REFERENCES

1. Romain Rolland, *Prophets of New India*, *op. cit.*, p. 340.
2. Quoted in S. Radhakrishnan (ed.), *Mahatma Gandhi*.
3. Sri Aurobindo, *The Ideal of Human Unity*, *op. cit.*, p. 69.
4. *Ibid.*, pp. 120-21.
5. *Ibid.*, pp. 287-88.
6. *Ibid.*, p. 36.
7. *Ibid.*, p. 323.
8. *Ibid.*, pp. 38-39.
9. Sri Aurobindo, *The Ideal of the Karmayogin*, *op. cit.*, p. 31.
10. Sri Aurobindo, *The Human Cycle*, *op. cit.*, p. 38.
11. *Ibid.*, pp. 39-40.
12. Sri Aurobindo, *Speeches*, *op. cit.*, p. 141.
13. *Ibid.*, pp. 29-30.
14. Sri Aurobindo, *The Uttarapara Speech*, *op. cit.*, p. 20.
15. V.P. Varma, *The Political Philosophy of Sri Aurobindo*, *op. cit.*, p. 208.
16. Sri Aurobindo, *The Ideal of the Karmayogin*, *op. cit.*, p. 18.
17. Sri Aurobindo, *Bankim-Tilak-Dayananda*, *op. cit.*, p.18.
18. Sri Aurobindo, *The Ideal of the Karmayogin*, *op. cit.*, pp. 5-6.
19. *Ibid.*, p. 11.
20. *Ibid.*, p. *4.*
21. *Message of Sri Aurobindo and the Mother*, pp. 22-23.
22. Sri Aurobindo, 'Letter on the Present Situation', *Advent*, 1950, pp. 90-91.
23. Hans Kohn, "Messianism", *Encyclopaedia of Social Sciences.*
24. Sri Aurobindo, *The Ideal of the Karmayogin*, *op. cit.*, p. 1.

25. J.C. Ghose, *Life-work of Sri Aurobindo Ghose, op. cit.*, p. 185.
26. Sri Aurobindo, 'The Indian Conception of Life', *Silver Jubilee Commemoration Volume of the Indian Philosophical Congress* (1950), pp. 173-79, p. 174.
27. Sri Aurobindo, *Speeches, op. cit.*, p. 45.
28. Sri Aurobindo, *The Doctrine of Passive Resistance, op. cit.*, pp. 78-79.
29. *Ibid.*, p. 81.
30. *Ibid.*, p. 87.
31. *Ibid.*, pp. 77-78.
32. *Ibid.*, pp. 62-65.
33. *Ibid.*, p. 65.
34. Sri Aurobindo, *More Lights on Yoga, op. cit.* p., 17.
35. Sri Aurobindo, *The Synthesis of Yoga, op. cit.*, p. 113.
36. Sri Aurobindo, *The Doctrine of Passive Resistance, op. cit.*, p. 53.
37. *Ibid.*, p. 79.
38. Sri Aurobindo, *Speeches, op. cit.*, pp. 173-74.
39. Sri Aurobindo, *The Ideal of Human Unity, op. cit.*, pp. 328-29.
40. *Ibid.*, p. 89.
41. *Ibid.*, p. 296.
42. *Ibid.*, p. 341.

BIBLIOGRAPHY

Works of Sri Aurobindo

The Ideal of Human Unity
Foundations of Indian Culture
The Spirit and Form of Indian Polity
The Human Cycle
The Doctrine of Passive Resistance
The Ideal of the Karmayogin
After the War
Speeches
Bankim-Tilak-Dayananda
The Renaissance in India
Ideals and Progress
The Superman
The Teaching and the Ashrama of Sri Aurobindo
Sri Aurobindo on himself and on the Mother
Evolution
The Problem of Rebirth
The Yoga and its Objects
A System of National Education
The Brain of India
Sri Aurobindo on India
War and Self-determination
Integral Yoga
Bankim Chandra Chatterjee

Works on Sri Aurobindo

Bali, D.R., *Modern Indian Thought*, Sterling Publishers, New

Delhi, 1980.

Briston, R., *Sri Aurobindo: Mystic*, Metaphysician, Poet.

Chaudhury, H., *Sri Aurobindo: The Prophet of Live Divine*, Sri Aurobindo Ashram, Pondicherry, 1951.

Chaudhury, H., *The Philosophy of Integralism*, Calcutta University D. Phil. Thesis.

Chaudhury, H., *Sri Aurobindo and the Meaning of Evolution.*

Chaudhury, H., and Spiegeberg, *Integral Philosophy of Sri Aurobindo*, London, 1960.

Das, A.C., *Sri Aurobindo and the Future of Mankind*, 1935.

Diwakar, R.R., *Mahayogi*, Bharatiya Vidya Bhavan, Bombay, 1954.

Donnelly, M., *Founding the Life Divine*, Rider & Company, London, 1955.

Dutt, C.C., *The Culture of India as envisaged by Sri Aurobindo*, Bharatiya Vidya Bhavan, Bombay, 1960.

Ghose, H.P., *Sri Aurobindo: The Prophet of Patriotism*, A.K. Mitter, Calcutta, 1949.

Gupta, N.K., *Sri Aurobindo and his Ashram*, Sri Aurobindo Ashram, Pondicherry, 1961.

Gupta, N.K., *The Message of Sri Aurobindo and the Ashram*, Sri Aurobindo Niketan, New Delhi, 1951.

Gupta, N.K., *The Yoga of Sri Aurobindo*, Sri Aurobindo Ashram, Pondicherry, 1958.

Gupta, R.C., *Great Political Thinkers—East and West*, Lakshmi Narain Agarwal, Agra, 1963.

Iyengar, K.R.S., *Sri Aurobindo: An Introduction*, Rao and Raghavan Publishers, Mysore, 1961.

Iyengar, K.R.S., *Sri Aurobindo: An Introduction*, Arya Publishing House, Calcutta, 1950.

Kartus, S., *Aurobindo: Prophet of Human Unity*, San Francisco, 1961.

Langley, G.H., *Sri Aurobindo: Poet, Philosopher and Mystic.*

Mahajan, V.D., *Modern Indian Political Thought*, S. Chand & Company, New Delhi, 1967.

Maitra, S.K., *Studies in Sri Aurobindo's Philosophy*, Banaras, 1945.

Maitra, S.K., *An Introduction to the Philosophy of Sri Aurobindo.*

Maitra, S.K., *The Meeting of the East and the West in Sri Aurobindo's Philosophy*, Pondicherry, 1956.

Mishra, R.S., *Integral Advaitism of Sri Aurobindo*, Banaras, 1957.

Mitra, S.K., *Sri Aurobindo and Indian Freedom*, Sri Aurobindo Library, Madras, 1948.

Mitra, S.K., *The Liberator*, Jaico, Bombay, 1954.

Mitra, S.K., *Sri Aurobindo and the New World*, Pondicherry, 1957.

Mukherjee, H., *Sri Aurobindo's Political Thought*, Firma, K.L. Mukhopadhyaya, Calcutta, 1957.

Mukherjee, S.L., The *Philosophy of Man-Making*, New Central Book Agency, Calcutta, 1971.

Pandit, M.P., *Sri Aurobindo: Studies in the Light of his Thought.*

Pandit, M.P., *The Teaching of Sri Aurobindo*, Pondicherry, 1959.

Patil, R., *Life of Aurobindo Ghosh.*

Pearson, N., *Sri Aurobindo and the Soul Quest of Man*, Allen and Unwin, 1952.

Purani, A.B., *Sri Aurobindo: Addresses on his Life and Teaching.*

Purani, A.B., *Life of Sri Aurobindo*, Pondicherry, 1960.

Purani, A.B., *Sri Aurobindo's Savitri: An Approach and a Study.*

Ranchan, S.P., *Sri Aurobindo as a Political Thinker*, Konark Publishers, Delhi. 1988.

Rishabchand, *The Integral Yoga of Sri Aurobindo.*

Roy, A.B., *Sri Aurobindo: Some Views on International Problems.*

Roy, A.B., *Sri Aurobindo and the New Age.*

Roy, D.K., *Among the Great*, Jaico, Bombay, 1950.

Roy, D.K., *Sri Aurobindo Came to Me.*

Sarma, D.S., *The Renaissance of Hinduism.*

Satprem, *Sri Aurobindo or the Adventure of Consciousness*, New York, 1964.

Sharma, R.N., *The Philosophy of Sri Aurobindo*, Meerut, 1963.

Singh, K., *Prophet of Indian Nationalism, A Study of the Political Thought of Sri Aurobindo Ghose*, George Allen and Unwin, 1963.

Srivastava, R.S., *Sri Aurobindo and Theories of Evolution*, Unpublished D. Litt. Thesis of the Patna University.

Tagore, R., *Salutation to Sri Aurobindo*, Pondicherry, 1956.

Verma, V.P., *The Political Philosophy of Sri Aurobindo*, Asia Publishing House, Bombay, 1960.

Magazines and Journals

Bulletin of Physical Education

Mother India

Sri Aurobindo Circle Annual

Sri Aurobindo Mandira Annual

The Advent

INDEX